W9-AEL-898

STAR SPANGLED

A GUIDE
TO AMERICA'S
NEW MICROBREWERIES
AND BREWPUBS

BEER

by Jack Erickson

RedBrick Press

RESTON, VIRGINIA

Although the author has extensively researched material to write this book, no guarantees can be made that all the information is complete or accurate. No responsibility can be assumed for errors, inaccuracies, omissions or any inconsistencies in the manuscript.

Star Spangled Beer: A Guide to America's New Microbreweries and Brewpubs. Copyright © 1987 by Jack Erickson. Printed and bound in the United States of America. All rights reserved. No part of this book may be reproduced in any form or by an electronic or mechanical means including information storage and retrieval systems without written permission in writing from the publisher, except by a reviewer, who may quote brief passages for a review.

First printing: April 1987
Second printing: November 1987

Cover design: Kevin Osborn, Research and Design Associates.
Cover photos: Mark Borchelt.

Published in 1987 in the United States of America by RedBrick Press, P.O. Box 2184, Reston, Virginia 22090.

Library of Congress Cataloging in Publication Data.

Erickson, Jack
      Star Spangled Beer: A Guide to America's New Microbreweries
      and Brewpubs.

      Bibliography
      Includes Index

      1. Directory of American and Canadian Microbreweries
      2. History of Brewing

Library of Congress Catalog Card Number
86-63993

ISBN 0-941397-00-9

Printed and Bound in the United States of America
10 9 8 7 6 5 4 3 2

To my parents . . .
who told me my first stories about
homebrewing on Grandad's farm in North
Dakota during Prohibition.

Acknowledgements

In March 1985, I was on vacation driving around the English countryside visiting villages, cathedrals and castles. One of the daily treats was stopping in quaint pubs for a pint of ale and lunch. During these visits, I talked with the publicans (pub "bartenders") about the tremendous difference between English ales and American beers.

Several publicans talked about an organization called The Campaign for Real Ale or CAMRA, a grassroots group started in the early 1970s to fight the monopoly of major English brewers. The movement led to a successful revival of real ale brewing and a restoration of historic pubs around England.

I bought the current CAMRA "Good Beer Guide" and picked up several earlier editions from the 1970s when CAMRA was just starting to grow as a national consumer movement. On the flight back to the U.S., I decided to write an article about CAMRA and its successful campaign to return "real ale" brewing to England.

During my research, I was referred to the American Homebrewers Association in Boulder and, in May 1985, went to the Great American Beer Festival in Denver. I wrote about the festival and the microbrewers for *The Washington Post,* and began writing a weekly column on microbrewing for *The Reston (VA) Times.* By the end of the year, I was working on an outline for a book that eventually became "Star Spangled Beer."

i

In July 1986, I left my job and drove cross-country with Sasha, my 13-year-old daughter, to California. For the rest of the year, I visited microbreweries on the West Coast, Canada and the Midwest and interviewed the microbrewers who were leading the brewing revolution. Without exception, the microbrewers expressed a zeal and enthusiasm that was truly infectious; they believe in what they are doing and care very much about the quality of their beer and how it is received by the public. I congratulate them for their success and wish them all well.

No book is the product of one person; it represents many people offering their knowledge, guidance and time. This book was fortunate to have had many people helping it along the way. These people include: John Cristea, Leo and Edna Erickson, Dr. Joseph Owades, Rolf Olness, Lee Tunkis, Lee and Becky Erickson, Jim and Diane Brandt, Dan Rappaport of Farragut Publishing, Kevin Osborn of Research and Design Associates, Marlene Hochberg and Randy Abreo of *Washington Technology,* Mark Borchelt, Bruce Boston of Wordsmith, Rebecca Friedberg, Charlie Papazian and Rob Cunov of the American Homebrewers Association, Dori Whitney of *Brewers Digest*, Greg Noonan, Phil Katz of the Beer Institute, Barbara Miller, Washington Independent Writers, and all the microbrewers mentioned in the book especially Bill and Marie Newman, Matthew Reich, Gary Heurich, Jim Koch, Fritz Maytag, Paul Shipman, Jim Kollar, Michael Healy, and Bill Owens.

A special appreciation goes to Marilyn McMorran who sat next to me in the pubs on our tour around England and who offered help in so many ways all during the research and writing of "Star Spangled Beer." Thanks, Marilyn.

Table of Contents

INTRODUCTION

A "microbrewing" revolution is going on in America.

From California to Maine, Georgia to Washington, small-scale "microbreweries" and "brewpubs" are reviving a cherished and historic American tradition — brewing specialty beers. (Microbreweries are small breweries producing approximately 15,000 barrels of beer or less per year; brewpubs are restaurants or taverns that brew beer on the premises.)

What started in 1977 in an old warehouse in Sonoma, California, with an ex-Navy sailor, Jack McAuliffe, retooling his homebrew equipment into the New Albion microbrewery, has grown in 10 years into a nationwide movement.

(Ninety miles south in San Francisco, appliance heir Fritz Maytag had bought the old Anchor Brewery in 1965 and begun to produce specialty beers such as Anchor Steam in the late 1960s. Some would argue that Maytag was the first microbrewer since he brewed beers commonly associated with microbreweries today. It was 12 years, however, until the next microbrewery appeared and there was a distinct difference between Maytag's venture and the microbreweries started by McAuliffe and his generation.)

(Maytag used family resources to revive a brewery; McAuliffe and other pioneering microbrewers were former homebrewers with meager finances who started microbrewing in warehouses, garages and industrial parks. The odds against McAuliffe's generation were awesome and many did not survive. Because there is such a difference between Maytag and McAuliffe's generation of microbrewers, this book considers the founding of the New Albion brewery as the birth of the micro-brewing movement. After all, microbrewing was incubating during the 12 years after Maytag bought Anchor until McAuliffe started New Albion. It literally exploded in the decade after New Albion began in 1977. This subjective judgment should, in no way, be considered a slight against Maytag and his unique venture; he has been a leader and inspiration for every microbrewer.)

EIGHTY MICROBREWERIES SPREAD ACROSS AMERICA AND CANADA

Today there are approximately 80 microbreweries and brewpubs in the U.S. and in Canada and about 15 more of these new breweries are planning to begin brewing in 1987. But those numbers are deceiving; although there are currently fewer than 100 microbreweries, the movement is growing rapidly and expanding into important markets in New York, San Francisco, Seattle, Washington, D. C., Boston and Philadelphia. The future for these small scale breweries appears more than promising — it portends a renaissance in brewing and appreciation for fine beer all over America.

Ten years after New Albion signaled the beginning of this renaissance, microbreweries are proving you don't have to be a big brewery to be successful; nor do you have to brew the same light pilsner beer so heavily advertised on TV. A small brewery in America can brew beer the old-fashioned way using just four ingredients — malted barley, hops, yeast and water — and find a market of appreciative beer drinkers. Some microbreweries have even been so bold as to brew specialty beers — ales, porters, stouts, bock and seasonal beers — that haven't regularly been brewed in America in decades.

Today the microbrewing movement ranges from Manhattan brew-pub restaurants a few blocks from Wall Street (New Amsterdam Brewery and Taproom and the Manhattan Brewing Company) to warehouse breweries in the Rocky Mountains (Hale's Ales in Colville, Washington; Kessler Brewing in Helena, Montana; Snake River in Caldwell, Idaho), to West Coast port cities of Seattle (Independent Ale and Kemper) and San Francisco (Anchor, San Francisco, Roaring Rock).

MICROBREWERS COME FROM MANY CALLINGS

One fascination with the microbrewing movement is the diverse backgrounds of the microbrewers themselves: Fritz Maytag was a graduate student at Stanford University before buying the nearly bankrupt Anchor Brewery in San Francisco; Jim Koch was a $200,000 per year management consultant who abandoned a lucrative career to start Boston Beer; Ken Grossman was a bicycle repairman before co-founding Sierra Nevada in Chico, California; Dick Bourke was a wine distributor who started Kessler in Helena, Montana; Tom Baune was a Weyerhaeuser forestry engineer before starting Hart Brewing with his wife in Kalama, Washington; Michael Healy was vice-president of a Chicago bank note firm that printed foreign currency before buying the failing Walter Brewery in Eau Claire, Wisconsin, to start Hibernia; Jim Kollar was a veterinarian before starting Chesapeake Bay Brewing Company in Virginia Beach, Virginia; Bill Owens was an award-winning photographer before he opened one of California's first brew-pubs in Hayward.

What these microbrewers had in common was professional success in their chosen career field; many had even become wealthy. None had formal training or education in brewing. Yet, at some point in their lives, the same thought occurred to all of them, "I want to start my own brewery!"

Once the seed was planted, it was a short time until they abandoned their careers for the high-risk world of microbrewing. They are, in every sense of the word, pioneers — true American entrepreneurs who saw a niche in the marketplace that was not being served. That market was specially brewed, high quality beers once common in America and still popular in Europe.

MICROBREWING IS THE FUTURE

The microbrewers' collective actions over the last 10 years have changed the course of brewing history in America.

With one exception, those microbrewing pioneers are enjoying a measure of success today. None is making big money yet, but they're patient; the movement is only a decade old. Their fruits will come in the future when microbrewing becomes a way of life instead of just an exciting new trend.

If you have not had the opportunity to try any microbrewed beers — a delight is waiting for you. One of these days, you'll walk into a liquor store or restaurant and see New Amsterdam, Anchor, Hibernia, Boulder, Samuel Adams, Sierra Nevada, Hart or some other microbrewed beers.

Be adventurous.

Do yourself a favor and try one.

Pour a glass and watch the rich, foamy head rise to the top. Put your nose up to the rim and take a sniff of the hoppy aroma exploding from the bubbles. Try to remember when you smelled such a luscious, pungent aroma from your ordinary beer.

Then take a sip and enjoy.

You may not be won over instantly, but be patient, these beers have more distinctive tastes than you're used to. But with a little time . . . and a few more tastings . . . you'll discover why so many people have been won over by the difference and why the microbrewing revolution is one of the most important trends in the food and beverage industry for the future.

They're here . . . the Star Spangled Beers.

In just ten years, microbreweries have become a part of America's brewing heritage that includes some of the most colorful chapters in the nation's history. That heritage includes the Pilgrims carrying beer aboard the Mayflower to the Founding Fathers retiring to a pub to celebrate the signing of the Declaration of Independence over a few pints of ale and on to the Golden Age of brewing in the 1870s when more than 4,000 breweries brewed beer in America.

And although the "Golden Age" of brewing may be gone . . . along with the 5-cent mug of beer and corner saloons selling buckets of beer . . . brewing is exciting once again — thanks to America's new microbreweries and their "Star Spangled Beers."

— *1* —

THE MICROBREWING
REVOLUTION

A revolution started in the summer of 1977 in an old warehouse on the outskirts of Sonoma, California, north of San Francisco.

In that sleepy town in the Northern California wine country, a 26-year-old ex-Navy electrician was assembling stainless steel tanks, pipes, kettles and bottling equipment he had scrounged from old dairies and junkyards.

His name was Jack McAuliffe, and he had a dream to take his homebrewing experience and build a small commercial brewery to brew ales like those he had drunk while stationed with the Navy in Scotland. McAuliffe's market was trend-conscious Californians searching for something distinctive in their food and beverages. He believed they were ready for beer that was not the bland, light lagers brewed by the major American breweries.

McAuliffe named his tiny microbrewery New Albion, and for a few years he brewed ales, porters and stouts that had not been brewed in America for decades.

McAuliffe was a pioneer; he had a vision and became America's first "microbrewer." But like other pioneers, McAuliffe's venture did not survive. His impact never got much beyond a novelty — a California eccentric hand-crafting beer without the financing, marketing, promotional or sales experience necessary to survive in a fiercely competitive marketplace. A lesson McAuliffe learned too late was that brewing beer is only half the game; the other half is selling beer. Lots of it.

In 1980, McAuliffe was forced to close New Albion and sell his equipment to another microbrewery north of Sonoma to pay bills and loans.

THE FIRST GENERATION OF MICROBREWERS

But by that time, other adventurous Californians were stepping in and trying their hand at microbrewing. In nearby Sacramento, Jim Schleuter started the River City Brewery; in Chico, Ken Grossman and Paul Camussi started Sierra Nevada; and in Marin County, fireman Mike DeBakker, started the DeBakker Brewery.

The microbrewing revolution also was exported to other Western states: Chuck Coury started the Cartwright Brewery in Portland and brewed an ale fermented with lager yeast; in Colorado, three home-brewers formed the Boulder Brewing Company and began producing English-style ales.

These pioneering microbrewers started with used dairy equipment and whatever they could pick up from old breweries and bottling plants. They cut corners by doing their own welding, electrical work, construction and plumbing. What they lacked in business acumen and experience they made up with enthusiasm, sweat, and zeal.

Along the way, they learned they were selling beer to people who had been drinking inexpensive and almost tasteless beer for years. Microbrewing pioneers frequently received an enthusiastic response locally to their beer, but they needed to expand their markets if they expected to continue as a commercial enterprise. A "cottage brewery" was charming and quaint, but it had little chance of survival unless it could sell volumes of beer regularly.

With the exception of Fritz Maytag, the first generation of micro-brewers could brew good beer, but knew little about selling it. To survive (not even thinking of prospering), they had to learn about raising capital, marketing, sales, promotion, advertising and distribution.

McAuliffe, Schleuter, DeBakker, Grossman, Camussi and Coury were the first generation of microbrewing pioneers. Although most did

not survive, they inspired future generations of microbrewing entrepreneurs who saw what *they* saw — a nation of beer drinkers eager
for distinctive taste in beers and willing to pay premium prices for them.

These early microbrewers were all homebrewers inspired by en-
trepreneurism and a vision that they could be successful just because
they were pioneers. Ten years later, only Sierra Nevada and Boulder
survive; the others, like meteors in the night sky, burned out as quickly
as they appeared.

The equipment from McAuliffe's New Albion brewery brews on
in the Mendocino Brewing Company's small brewpub in Hopland, a
hundred miles north of Sonoma. But more important, McAuliffe's
dream lives on in almost 100 microbreweries and brewpubs across the
U.S. and Canada.

THE SECOND DECADE OF MICROBREWING

Although the 10-year-old microbrewing movement is still in its
infancy, it is rapidly growing in numbers, popularity, variety and consumer awareness.

Production from all microbreweries and brewpubs is still very
small — less than 1% of domestic beer production. But growth since
1984 indicates that microbreweries may duplicate the popularity of
imported beers in the U.S. in a few years, now about 6% of gross sales
or about 8 million barrels per year.

Today's microbrewing revolution is significant in many ways:

1) Microbreweries generally originate from the grassroots, i.e.,
small partnerships or "mom-and-pop" enterprises with limited capital
and business experience.

2) Microbreweries brew specialty beers with only traditional ingredients of malted barley, hops, yeast and water and do not use cereal
grain adjuncts such as corn and rice as major brewers do to make
lighter, thinner beer.

3) The variety of beers brewed by microbreweries (traditional
lagers, steam beers, porters, ales, stouts, bocks) is more typical of what
can be found in the major European brewing countries of England,
Belgium and Germany.

4) Microbrewed beers are aimed not at the traditional Budweiser,
Miller or Coors drinkers, but at the affluent, trend-setting consumers
who have become import and super-premium beer drinkers.

5) Microbrewers are generally enthusiastic and visionary entrepreneurs who have been creative in perceiving local market demand and starting neighborhood brewpubs and beer gardens or finding new and different ways to get their beer into the marketplace.

As microbrewing enters its second decade, it has become a national movement. It is flourishing in trend-setting northern California and the Northwest and has, since 1985, formed beachheads in East Coast urban centers and the Midwest. There are approximately 55 microbreweries and brewpubs in the U.S. today and that number is projected to approach 100 by 1988 with new microbreweries opening from Hawaii and Alaska to Vermont and Georgia.

THE SECOND GENERATION OF MICROBREWERS

A second generation of microbrewers began emerging in the early 1980s far from California.

Matthew Reich (Old New York Brewing, New York), Paul Shipman (Independent Ale, Seattle) and Jim Kollar (Chesapeake Bay Brewing, Virginia) started breweries via different methods. Reich became a "contract brewer" by hiring Dr. Joseph Owades and contracting to brew New Amsterdam Amber Beer at the West End Brewery in Utica, New York, to sell in Manhattan. Shipman built a small brewery mainly from used equipment. Kollar bought property and new brewing equipment, imported a German brewer and built a brewery from the ground up.

Today, Reich and Shipman are two of the most successful microbrewers in America. In October 1985, Reich opened The New Amsterdam Brewery and Taproom in Manhattan; Shipman's Redhook Ale has won wide acceptance as a unique and highly-rated beer.

Kollar, on the other hand, sold out in 1986 to an Exxon marketing executive, Michael Hollingsworth, after failing to market Chesbay successfully in five states with limited capital and far-flung distribution.

An important distinction about second-generation microbrewers Reich, a former Citibank lending officer, veterinarian Kollar and former winery salesman Shipman, is that they were already successful in other careers. Their prior business experience had taught them that there was more to brewing than just designing and manufacturing a product. They were more concerned about penetrating a market that they believed could support their venture. As a result, many second-generation microbrewers like Reich and Shipman have succeeded because they were more than brewers — they were marketers; they know how to sell their beer and consistently develop new markets.

During the early 1980s, the microbrewing revolution also reached such out-of-the-way areas as Caldwell, Idaho; Plano, Texas; Little Rock, Arkansas; Helena, Montana; and Albany, New York.

Another important part of this second wave was the emergence of brewpubs in California and Washington. Bert Grant started the first brewpub in America (Yakima Brewing and Malting, Yakima) in 1982, using his 40 years brewing experience to brew prize-winning English-style ales.

In California, Bill Owens (Buffalo Bill's Microbrewery, Hayward) and Michael Laybourn (Mendocino Brewing, Hopland) opened brew-pubs in 1983 after the legislature changed the law to permit a restaurant or tavern to brew and sell beer. Within three years, brewpubs were popping up around Northern California in Santa Cruz, San Francisco, Berkeley, Petaluma, and Sacramento.

FRITZ MAYTAG AND THE ANCHOR BREWING COMPANY

If there is a "guru" of the American microbrewing movement it is Fritz Maytag of the San Francisco Anchor Brewing Company. Since 1965 when Maytag purchased the run-down Anchor brewery while a Stanford Asian studies graduate student, he has paved the way by learning all the lessons of brewing a specialty beer, marketing it successfully and setting a standard for other microbrewers to follow.

The personable and articulate Maytag has also become an unofficial spokesman for the microbrewing movement, even though his brewery's production (1985: 38,000 barrels) technically takes Anchor out of the category of microbrewery.

(The benchmark used to classify microbreweries is annual production of 15,000 barrels per year or less. Production higher than 15,000 barrels/year usually qualifies one as a regional brewery. For the purposes of this book, however, a microbrewery is one that has limited production and also brews distinctive beers with traditional brewing techniques.)

(Anchor brews Anchor Steam, Porter, Wheat and Celebration Ale; Hibernia in Eau Claire, Wisconsin, brews All-Malt lager, Dunkel-

Weizen, Bock, and Oktoberfest. Brewing specialty beers is of more significance than the annual production of a brewery. That means breweries such as Anchor and Hibernia can be considered microbreweries even though both produce more than 15,000 barrels/year.)

Today, Anchor's beers are sold in liquor stores and restaurants around the country and are considered world-class gourmet beers. The brewery is also in a class by itself, with its shiny copper kettles, modern brewing equipment, wood paneling, and classic hospitality room.

Maytag manages his brewery staff like a small family. Unlike other breweries which operate around the clock, the Anchor Brewery runs only eight hours a day, five days a week. In the late summer, the brewery closes for a couple of days so the staff can travel with Maytag to a West Coast farm to observe the harvest of the special barley crop used for brewing Anchor's Christmas Ale.

For anyone who appreciates fine beer, a trip to San Francisco would not be complete without touring the Anchor Brewery on Mariposa Street south of Market Street. Quaffing a glass of fresh Anchor beer in the hospitality room after a tour of the brewery ranks with a visit to Chinatown when visiting the City by the Bay. Neither should be missed.

DIVERSITY IN MICROBREWING

Microbrewing shares something in common with the 1960s Chinese Cultural Revolution; both experienced a period of "let a hundred flowers bloom." Microbrewing is still enjoying that creative flourishing with almost every microbrewery different from the others. That remains part of the charm of microbreweries; they are not "homogenized" by any means. They usually represent the dreams and hopes of their founder who has very definite ideas about how to brew and market beer.

Of the 55 microbreweries and brewpubs in America, there are only a few which resemble each other in any way. In fact, most are highly individualistic enterprises reflecting the personality and vision of their founder in 1) brewing, 2) product identity, and 3) marketing.

The one concept all the microbreweries share is identifying with a local area and its customs or heritage. For example, the founders of Montana Brewing in Helena purchased the rights to the Kessler name to take advantage of the connection to the historic Kessler Brewery, founded by two gold prospectors in Helena (then known as Last Chance Gulch) when Montana was a territory. The founders of California's Xcelsior Brewery did the same when they purchased the rights to the Acme name from the old Acme Brewery, which was one of the largest in California after Prohibition.

Other examples of breweries associating with a local area include Boulder Brewing's use of the Flatiron Mountains and Sierra Nevada illustrating the Sierra Nevada peaks on their labels. Seattle's Independent Ale even named one of their beers after the local neighborhood and put a Scandinavian expression, "Ya sure, ya betcha!" and a picture of a Norwegian on the label of their Ballard Bitter.

This may be just normal marketing; it also recognizes that these breweries want to be considered local breweries with personalities all their own and shun aspirations about being anything more than the "hometown" beer. If their beer is popular outside their area, well, that's very nice, but it just shows that others also have good taste and appreciate fine beer.

TWO MICROBREWERS

Another example of diversity within the microbrewing industry extends to how they approach brewing. Two extremes would be the personalities behind Boston Beer Company and Saxton's Brewery.

Jim Koch (Boston Beer Company) is a sophisticated, Harvard-educated businessman who hired a consultant to help him brew on contract Samuel Adams Boston Lager (even though Samuel Adams never tasted a lager). Koch sells thousands of barrels of his beer on the East Coast and had the marketing and promotional savvy to win "Most Popular Beer" in America for two years in a row.

Dewayne Saxton (Saxton Brewing Company, Chico, California) is also a microbrewer like Koch, but brews in his basement and bottles by hand a hundred barrels of Ivanhoe Ale a year.

Koch is a genius at marketing and aggressive promotion; Saxton is a craftsman who approaches brewing like an Old-World artisan. There is room for both in microbrewing, but it is misleading to lump them in the same category as "microbrewers" without understanding the many ways they differ in their approach to brewing and selling beer. Saxton could learn lessons from Koch about marketing beer; Koch could also benefit from Saxton's approach to the intricacies of small-scale brewing.

CATEGORIES OF MICROBREWERIES

To describe the complexity of microbrewing — and to do justice to microbrewers themselves — distinctions should be made between their various types. The following categories describe their diversity:

Craft brewer — small scale production, fewer than 3,000 barrels annually, with limited distribution or marketing (Saxton Brewery, Chico, California, 100 barrels in 1985);

Specialty brewer — a microbrewer with larger production (up to 15,000 barrels per year) and marketing in a regional area (Independent Ale, Seattle);

Contract brewer — a brewer who uses the facilities of a larger brewery and is basically involved in marketing (Jim Koch, Boston Beer Company, brews at Pittsburgh Brewing Company). A contract brewer may have plans to build his own brewery such as Matthew Reich has done in Manhattan with his New Amsterdam Brewery;

Pubbrewer (brewpub) — a brewer who brews and retails at a tavern or restaurant (Bill Owens, Buffalo Bill's Microbrewery, Hayward, California). In most cases, the brewpub is the sole outlet for the in-house brewery.

Although microbreweries have diverse methods of brewing and marketing, they share a common goal — brewing high quality beers using only malted barley, hops, yeast and water. A few use the shortcut of brewing with malt extract, a syrup made from malting barley. Those who do are identified as malt extract brewers.

Microbrewers also eschew the practice of major brewers who dilute and weaken their beer by using corn and rice adjuncts. These adjuncts produce the lighter, thinner pilsner beer advertised so heavily on TV. Several microbreweries produce wheat beers in the summer, but these are considered specialty beers since the wheat is malted like barley in brewing traditional beers.

THE THIRD GENERATION — FUTURE MICROBREWERS

Already within the microbrewing movement, a new type of microbrewery is emerging somewhat distinct from the first and second generations. This third generation is already benefiting from the lessons of earlier generations.

An example of this new generation of microbrewers is Jim Brock of the Koolau Brewery in Hawaii. Brock and his partners have raised $2 million and are raising another $2 million before they begin brewing. Early in their venture, Brock and his partners did a market survey of Honolulu and determined that a profitable microbrewery could succeed in the small Hawaiian market (360 square miles) and not worry about selling "off island."

The Brock venture is more a second-generation microbrewery than first-generation because its emphasis is on marketing, with every phase of operations overseen by professionals (such was not the case in most earlier microbrewing ventures). This early emphasis on marketing has paid off well for Brock and his partners; Honolulu hotels, liquor stores and restaurants have already purchased the first year's production of the Koolau Brewery.

The difference between second-generation microbrewers and third-generation is that the latter likely will raise more money (upwards of $3 million) and target an affluent urban area (such as Atlanta, Miami, Los Angeles, Chicago or Houston) where there is presently no microbrewery. The third generation will also have considerable professional expertise on hand from the beginning of the venture including a lawyer, an accountant, and marketing, sales and brewing representatives. A nucleus of experienced business talent is increasingly recognized as necessary for the high-risk world of microbrewing. Professional expertise and management are also critical for raising venture capital.

THE AMERICAN HOMEBREWERS ASSOCIATION

Microbrewing is really an offshoot of the homebrewing movement, which experienced a reawakening in the late 1970s after President Carter signed legislation making it legal for each adult to brew 100 gallons of beer per year at home. Until then, homebrewing technically had been illegal since Prohibition because of a technical oversight in federal regulations drawn up after Repeal. Nevertheless, homebrewing had become a popular hobby for thousands of normally law-abiding citizens.

Since the days of New Albion, microbreweries have been supported and encouraged by the American Homebrewers Association (AHA) of Boulder, Colorado. Charlie Papazian, President of the AHA, is himself a pioneer who has seen homebrewing evolve into a national movement of 1½ million homebrewers with local groups active in all regions of the country.

Papazian and the AHA staff publish brewing magazines (Zymurgy and The New Brewer), books (Brewers Publications) and conduct regional and national conferences including the popular annual Great American Beer Festival. AHA has also established an education group, the Association of Brewers, to further the cause of microbrewing and homebrewing in North America.

THE FUTURE OF MICROBREWING

Brewing consultants, equipment manufacturers and brewing suppliers in the U.S., Great Britain and Canada are already catering to the microbrewing industry. They, like others observing the industry, recognize that the future is very promising for microbreweries and brewpubs.

Although there may be a limit on the number of microbreweries that will likely emerge (largely confined to urban areas of one-half million population or university towns), the number and type of brewpubs are almost unlimited.

A major city such as Boston, Atlanta, Washington or Chicago may support only one or two microbreweries, but could be the home for several brewpubs. Popular tourist states such as Massachusetts, North Carolina, Arizona, Washington and Oregon could support many brewpubs. But the largest potential for brewpubs is in populous states like California, Florida and New York.

Bill Owens, owner of Buffalo Bill's Microbrewery, has observed, "In 10 years, you'll be able to drive all the way up the California coast from San Diego to Eureka and never be more than 10 minutes from a brewpub."

There may be a slight exaggeration in Owens' prediction, but his point is well made; brewpubs have the potential to become a substantial share of the multi-billion-dollar restaurant trade in North America over the next decade. Owens is not the only one who recognizes the potential for brewpubs in California. In that trend-setting state, some 25 restaurants, inns and taverns are considering installing equipment to brew beer and become brewpubs.

With that much activity and interest, it will not be long before major food and beverage corporations see the potential of brewpubs and enter the field. Look for the first chain of brewpubs to start in Northern California and move up the Northwest Coast where existing microbreweries and brewpubs have already laid the groundwork by brewing their specialty beers. With consumers already familiar with microbrewed beer, restaurants and taverns along the West Coast are likely to install brewpub equipment and reap the harvest.

The Midwest and East Coast will probably have their first brewpub chains in the 1990s after the concept has flourished on the West Coast. The positive aspect of brewpub chains is that freshly brewed beer will be more widely available to Americans who haven't experienced the microbrewing revolution. Let's hope the quality of the beer does not suffer in the mass marketing.

★　　★　　★

— 2 —

THE EARLY HISTORY OF BEER

SOMEWHERE IN A CAVE . . . FAR AWAY AND A LONG TIME AGO . . .

Imagine, if you will, a tribe of European cavemen ten thousand years ago returning from a hunt for game for the long winter.

When the cavemen entered their damp cave, they made a discovery; clay pots of grain stored from the fall harvest had become soaked with moisture. When the cavemen took a few sips of this malty beverage, they were soothed by its freshness and taste. Instead of throwing out the beverage, they kept it to drink after hunts and with meals.

Eventually, the cavemen discovered there was more to this beverage than just a refreshing taste and aroma; when they drank it, the beverage gave them a pleasant, relaxed feeling. And when they drank large amounts of it, they felt exhilarated and could even tolerate their fellow tribesmen a bit more. Life just seemed a little more bearable when there was some of this curious beverage to drink around their fires at night after hunting mastodons and fleeing saber-toothed tigers.

So refreshing was this malty beverage that the cavemen regularly began setting aside pots of grain soaked in water. To experiment, they added herbs to create different tastes. Before long, they were planting additional crops in the summer to brew this beverage in the fall.

The particulars of the discovery of malted beverages or beer — by whom, where, and when — are, unfortunately, lost to history. It most likely happened by accident. And although it may not have the significance as the discovery of fire or the invention of the wheel, the discovery by early man of the qualities of malted beverages had an effect upon civilization that continues to this day.

FROM THE DAWN OF CIVILIZATION

Beer is as old as civilization itself.

Whenever grain and water are mixed and left for a period of time, fermentation takes place. Yeast, or tiny microorganisms that cause fermention, are present everywhere — particularly in musty, damp places like caves.

Although no one knows when the first fermented grain beverage was brewed by design, Mesopotamian clay tablets dating from 6000 B.C. make the first reference to brewing. In the Mesopotamian city of Ur Hippur, Queen Shubad drank beer from a golden tube, which was buried in her tomb and found by 20th century archeologists.

Beer was brewed widely in Egypt several thousand years before Christ was born and along the banks of the Tigris and Euphrates Rivers where modern civilizations first emerged. The Egyptians, who grew many different grains, worshiped Isis as the goddess of both fertility and brewing.

Beer was mentioned in the 5,000-year-old "Book of the Dead," the record of early Egyptian kings. Hieroglyphics from temple walls show how the Egyptians brewed beer and workers who built the Pyramids drank beer as their main beverage.

When Hammurabi was King of Babylon 4,000 years ago, he wrote laws governing the price and conditions for the sale of beer (payment to be made in corn). Brewers who diluted their brews were imprisoned in their own vats.

An Assyrian tablet from 2000 B.C. recorded Noah as carrying beer aboard the Ark. Several books in the Old Testament (Genesis, Leviticus, Nehemiah, and Ecclesiastes) also refer to barley wine, a form of beer.

Beer was also brewed in India and China with rice, barley, wheat and millet. One form of Chinese beer was called *Kiu,* which meant it was yellow and sparkling. Another form of Chinese beer was made from rice and called *zythum.*

Although Romans preferred the fruit of the grape, the word "beer" is derived from the Latin word *bibere* (to drink). The Spanish word *cervesa* comes from Ceres, the Roman goddess of agriculture.

When the wine-drinking Romans invaded England, they found Celts had already introduced a fermented beverage called *curmi*. Beer drinking survived the Romans in the British Isles, and during Anglo-Saxon times the name "ale" emerged, a corruption of the Norse word *ol*.

Scandinavians sang of beer in their sagas and legends. The Finnish saga, Kalevala, tells how they brewed their beer 1,000 years before Christ. The early Norsemen sang of their beer, called *bjor,* as passionately as they did of slaughtering their enemies. An early Norse epic poem boasts of vanquishing foes and drinking ale from their skulls.

In medieval Europe, brewing beer and baking bread went together in the same kitchens. Since women were bakers in these early kitchens, they were also the first brewers. Only later in the 17th century, when brewing became a successful commercial enterprise, did men take over from women the role of brewers.

Beer has been called "liquid bread" since both products contain the same ingredients — grain, water and yeast. Early beers and ales did not contain hops but frequently had herbs such as sage, bog myrtle, ground ivy, and cedar added for flavoring.

Fermented beverages were drunk by all ages and classes of people in medieval Europe. The fermentation actually provided a healthier drink than water because alcohol killed small amounts of bacteria. Water supplies were frequently polluted in early towns and cities because sanitation was crude. Thus, mildly alcoholic ale became a common beverage drunk by men, women and children all during the day and night.

BREWING IN GERMANY

Early on, German states and cities, particularly in the North, became leaders in brewing. More than 1,000 brewmasters were registered in Hamburg in 1376, and Einbeck became Germany's most famous brewing city and shipped its beer to other European cities.

Throughout Germany, monasteries became centers for brewing. Bavarian monks in the 15th century stored beer in the summer in wooden casks in Alpine caverns. The word lager comes from the German verb *lagern,* "to store."

In 1516, the Duke of Bavaria decreed the famous Reinheitsgebot, a purity law dictating that beer could only be made from barley, hops and water. (Yeast was not mentioned in the law since the role of this important microorganism was unknown.) This purity law still stands today in Germany, and brewers in other countries take pride when they say they brew their beer "according to the Reinheitsgebot." (A Texas microbrewery even adopted the Reinheitsgebot name for its brewery).

At the beginning of the 16th century in Europe, hops were discovered as a mild and flavorful ingredient that would impart a robust aroma and taste to beer. Hops also slowed contamination from wild yeasts and bacteria that flourished wherever beer was brewed and stored. After the discovery of these important characteristics, the hop "weed" soon became a plant cultivated in Europe as a necessary ingredient in beer.

BREWING IN EARLY ENGLAND

Like Germany, England became a nation that took brewing seriously. Early Celtic tribes brewed beer and the first reference to an English ale house dates to 296 A.D. Alehouses were so popular that they became inns for travelers in need of rest, a meal, and fresh ale.

As in Germany, monasteries (until Henry VIII in the early 16th century) were the first centers of brewing in England. When Thomas à Becket made his journey to the King of France in 1157, he took along a cask of ale from the Canterbury monastery.

In the 35th article of the Magna Carta granted by King John in 1215, wine and ale were referred to in a section on precise weights and measures.

During Henry III's reign in the 13th century, ale was such a part of commerce that its price was fixed along with the price of wine and grain.

Ale was as much a drink of royalty in England as it was for commoners. Queen Elizabeth I (1533-1603) drank her share of beer and gave a large daily beer allowance to her ladies-in-waiting. The women in Henry VIII's court were allowed a gallon of beer for breakfast!

The debate over adding hops to ale in England eventually became a matter of state concern; it was forbidden until as late as 1556. Even after hops were allowed, Henry VIII ordered brewers not to use hops in the ales he drank.

Trevelyan's *History of England* includes a reference to the hop controversy in a short verse:

Hops, Reformation, bays and beer
Came into England all in one year.

But in time, hops became more widely used in English ales when their ability to retard souring, as well as to impart a mild bitterness, became more popular.

By 1730, a new style of ale called "porter" was becoming popular in England. Early porter was a mixture of ale and stout, a dark, heavy ale usually drunk in the colder months. In pubs all over London, customers would order porter by asking for "'alf 'n' 'alf," or a pint of half ale and half stout. The name porter was derived from the popularity of the drink with London porters. Eventually, a London brewer brewed porter using ingredients of both ale and stout.

BREWING REACHES THE INDUSTRIAL AGE

Throughout 17th century Europe, brewing evolved from a "cottage" or monastery activity into a commercial enterprise. Once brewing had been done in the home by women called brewsters or alewives. But when brewing become a lucrative commercial activity, "alewives" were replaced by men who became professional "brewers."

Pubs were the original breweries in England until the 1700s, when the first commercial breweries (Whitbread, Charrington, Courage, Truman and Ind) appeared. London breweries became prosperous and grew rapidly because they were able to brew large volumes of fresh beer for the emerging class of English industrial workers.

The industrial age also came to breweries when they began using steam power for everything from grinding grain to heating the brew-kettle. Science also improved the quality of beer by treating water chemically to produce more distinctive, lighter ales and darker porters and stouts.

One of the greatest advances in brewing was Louis Pasteur's discovery in 1875 of the function of yeast in fermenting beer. The once happenstance activity of pitching yeast into wort became a rigidly scientific process as hydrometers, thermometers and microscopes were used to improve fermentation. Beer now could be brewed year-round — not just in cool weather. The consistency and quality of beer improved dramatically.

How beer was served also underwent changes during the industrial revolution. When glassblowing became a commercial activity, beer could be kept in smaller containers than the unwieldy wooden casks.

When the industrial age came to brewing, the importance of pub brewing declined as commercial brewers could ship beer to pubs all over the country. The improvements in the consistency and quality of beer forced many pubs to quit brewing and start carrying commercially brewed beer. This shift from pub brewing to large-scale commercial brewing eventually led to the "tied houses" in England with pubs merely becoming outlets for commercial brewers.

But by this time, beer was more than just a European phenomenon. It had been a beverage common in the New World before Columbus found natives drinking a fermented beverage made from corn or maize. In the New World, beer was about to become the most American of all beverages.

3

BEER IN AMERICAN HISTORY

There was beer in America before the first explorers landed on our shores.

When Christopher Columbus was exploring the Caribbean Islands in the 1490s, he discovered Indians drinking a fermented beverage made from the maize or corn native to the New World. The Indians would put maize into a clay pot, pour in sap from a birch tree and fill with water. Wild yeast fermented the mixture into a dark beer that probably tasted spicy.

The first reference to brewing by early settlers in the New World was in 1587 when an English explorer, Richard Hakulyt, wrote that ale made from Virginia corn was as good as English ale. Barley for brewing was planted as early as 1605 in Virginia.

When the Pilgrims landed in 1620 at Plymouth, a logbook noted they chose Massachusetts instead of Virginia because they were running out of beer: " . . . we could not now take time for further search or consideration, our victuals being much spent, especially our beere." The Mayflower sailors even urged the Pilgrims immediately to search for fresh water as soon as they went ashore so they could preserve the little beer they had for the return trip to England.

In 1623, the Virginia Assembly urged immigrants to the New World to bring along malted barley to get their homebrewing batches started.

The first governor of Massachusetts, John Winthrop, brought 10,000 gallons of beer with him in 1629; he also urged government control of the consumption of spirits. By 1634, colonial taverns (or "ordinaries") were licensed and hours of operation restricted.

In a letter John Smith of Virginia wrote in 1629, he described how colonists were malting Indian corn to make a good ale.

By 1640, most colonial households made beer from bread with a bit of wild hops thrown into the brew. But the New World colonists were not the first to use the shortcut of brewing beer from bread; early civilizations did the same to save the time required to malt barley.

EARLY AMERICAN BREWING CENTERS

Breweries were prevalent in early colonial towns because beer was a healthier drink than water. Sanitation was crude in those days and water was distributed to homes via complicated networks of wooden pipes which would leak or break down. Water supplies frequently were contaminated and diseases common.

Beer, on the other hand, contained just enough alcohol to kill some bacteria. Thus, beer or ale was preferred by men, women and even children.

Boston, New Amsterdam (New York) and Philadelphia were cities where brewing were established as a main form of commerce and trade. Captain Robert Sedgwick, a founder of the Massachusetts Military Company, became America's first commercial brewer when he opened a brewhouse in the 1630s in Charlestown, a part of old Boston. Sedgwick even endowed tiny Harvard College in 1647 with a "shop" (a small brewhouse).

Brewing was an important part of life at Harvard, even when the college had only 100 students. Harvard's first President, Nathanial Easton, was dismissed in 1639 for a number of charges including not providing enough beer or bread to students (the beer ration was two pints at both daily meals provided by the college). Early students at Harvard even paid part of their tuition with wheat and malt.

The Dutch were even more zealous about brewing than the English; the Dutch West India Company started a brewery in 1632 on "Brouwers (Brewers) Straet" in New Amsterdam (New York).

New Amsterdam became the first cosmopolitan town in the colonies and breweries were an integral part of its commerce. Dutch brewers even sold beer to Virginia colonists and exported to the Netherlands.

Early Dutch brewers such as Jacob Kip (Kip's Bay) were men of wealth and authority. Peter Minuit, who bought Manhattan Island from the Indians in 1626, established the first pub in North America in 1622. Early New Amsterdam landmarks were the White Horse Tavern and the Red Lion Brewery; the City Tavern eventually became New York's first City Hall.

Although Pennsylvania was settled after Massachusetts and New York, brewing was one of the first considerations of William Penn. When he built his Bucks County estate at Pennsbury, he included a brewhouse that survived until 1864, more than 150 years after Penn died in 1718. Several breweries opened in Philadelphia; Pennsylvania beer was even exported to Barbados.

OUR FOUNDING FATHERS — BREWERS ALL

George Washington, Samuel Adams, Thomas Jefferson, Patrick Henry and Benjamin Franklin were all affiliated with brewing in some way.

George Washington had his own brewhouse at Mount Vernon and frequently sent brewing recipes to friends. A letter Washington wrote in 1737 while a colonel in the Virginia militia contains his recipe for "small beer," a type of homebrew. The handwritten letter is on display at the New York City Public Library.

Washington was partial to "porter," a dark, bitter beer imported from England. Porter was a bastardized blend of ale, stout and "two-penny" (or small beer) that publicans (English bartenders) poured from three separate casks. Although porter had become popular in England since it was introduced in the 1720s, it didn't have a large following in the colonies. Nevertheless, a friend of Washington's, Robert Hare, became a brewer of porter in Philadelphia.

Early American brewers were frequently men of wealth and power. Since England was taxing many foods and specialty goods — including molasses, beer and malting products — colonial brewers were active in the American Revolution. Prior to going to Valley Forge in November 1777, George Washington made the home of a wealthy Philadelphia brewer, George Emlen, headquarters for his Revolutionary Army.

During the Revolutionary War, American troops were to receive a daily ration of a quart of ale per day. Washington even wrote to Congress when his troops' ale ration was running out. But the Americans were not the only ones short of beer; the British were forced to have porter, beer, barley and other supplies sent by ship from England only to have pirates seize the ships and hand over their booty to Washington's troops.

Early brewers experimented with spices in their brews. Spruce beer was common, as was beer made with coriander seed, ginger, cinnamon and a "bitter bean." Pumpkin ale was brewed by adventurous brewers, but it had an strange "twang" and left a harsh taste. Peaches were also used to brew beer.

The changes taking place in brewing and drinking in Europe found their way to the colonies. The traditional wooden tankard drinking vessel was replaced first by pewter, then silver. Beer and ale became more marketable when companies began manufacturing glass containers.

BEER AS A DRINK OF MODERATION

Trade with the Caribbean Islands in the 18th century led to the import of rum and molasses into the colonies. By the Revolutionary War, rum and brandy (or "spirits" as they were called) were growing in popularity, much to the disappointment of religious organizations. Beer and ale were lower in alcohol and considered drinks of moderation. Temperance groups protested the distilling of "spirits" and the many evils they caused.

Dr. Benjamin Rush, a signer of the Declaration of Independence and Professor of Medicine at the University of Pennsylvania, wrote a pamphlet in 1775, "An Inquiry Into the Effects of Ardent Spirits upon the Human Body and Mind." The pamphlet, which became a leading document among the temperance movement, described the clinical effects of spirits and prescribed wine, beer and cider as healthier alternatives.

The General Court of Massachusetts passed an act in 1789 encouraging the manufacturing of beer "as an important means of preserving the health of citizens of this Commonwealth and of preventing the pernicious effects of 'spirituous liquors.' " New Hampshire went so far as to pass a law exempting from all taxes anyone who built a brewhouse.

BREWING AS AN EARLY INDUSTRY

In Alexander Hamilton's first report as Secretary of the Treasury in 1791, he noted brewing as an exemplary manufacturing industry for the young nation. Hamilton encouraged competition among brewers to promote growth in the industry; breweries were even given protective trade benefits.

The earliest tabulation of American breweries comes from a 1810 Secretary of Treasury report; there were 132 breweries (total value, $955,791) producing annually 185,000 barrels. Pennsylvania led with 48 breweries, followed by 42 in New York and 13 in Ohio.

Although Philadelphia and New York were still brewing centers, the industry suffered a decline after 1810 along with other industries. America was becoming a heavy consumer of imported goods, and brewers filed reports in the 1820 census that said, "Sales diminished," and "Dull."

After Thomas Jefferson retired as President in 1809, he returned to his Monticello estate and became interested in brewing. He read many books, talked with local brewers, and built a brewhouse.

In a letter to a businessman who had once tried to get the American government to start a national brewery, Jefferson wrote that he encouraged the growth of breweries as an alternative to the rum and whiskey industries. Jefferson also wrote, "I am lately become a brewer for family use, having had the benefit of instruction of an English brewer of the first order."

Jefferson took a keen interest in his small brewery, writing to merchants requesting bottles and corks which were in short supply. He even invited James Madison to Monticello for the fall brewing. Jefferson brewed 100 gallons of ale in the fall and another 100 in the spring; he received praise on his ales and had many requests for his recipes.

By the time Jefferson died in 1825, American brewing had plummeted. The number of breweries in America was declining and rum and whiskey were more popular. Two important developments were also happening: the temperance movement was growing, and the nation's taste in beer was undergoing a dramatic change from ales to a German style of beer called lager.

EARLY TEMPERANCE MOVEMENTS

Although the first national temperance association was formed in 1826, its roots went back to earlier times. The original focus of temperance groups was against "strong spirits" such as brandy, rum and whiskey. The consumption of beer, cider, malt liquor and wine was actually encouraged. Temperance actually stood for moderation; total abstinence from alcohol did not become a rallying cry for another fifty years.

The original temperance movement was started by men of religion, many from universities. The movement's homeland was New England, home of the Puritans who espoused social propriety, abstention, and moral severity.

The movement grew quickly. By the end of 1829, 100,000 had joined; by 1833, 1.5 million. Chapters started in cities all around the country with support coming from legislatures, Congress, colleges and factories.

At a national convention in 1833, the movement changed its name to the United States Temperance Union; in 1836 to the American Temperance Union. At this convention, total abstinence was proclaimed.

The movement rapidly progressed from espousing moderation . . . to abstinence . . . to prohibition; by the 1840s, the movement was calling for prohibiting the sale of all liquor. In Maine, the nation's first prohibition law was passed and signed by the governor in 1851. The Maine law became the model for similar acts passed by Minnesota, Rhode Island, Massachusetts, Vermont, Connecticut, New York, New Hampshire, Delaware, Indiana and Iowa.

All of the state prohibition laws eventually were declared unconstitutional or were repealed.

The strength of the state temperance movements alarmed the brewing and liquor industries. But the brewers and distillers got a temporary respite from the fury of zealous prohibitionists when the momentum generated in the states was spent and the movement was stifled. It was 25 years before another state passed a prohibition law.

GERMAN LAGER BEERS

Just as porter changed the tastes in English brewing in the 18th century, another beer changed America's taste in the 19th century. That change was from English-style ale to German-style lager.

This change began in the 1840s when the first wave of German immigrants began arriving on America's shores. Many of these Germans were brewers who brought a yeast different from that used to ferment English ales, stouts and porters.

The immigration of Germans to America in the mid-1800s occurred simultaneously with the growth of Philadelphia, New York, Cincinnati, St. Louis, Chicago and Milwaukee. The first lager brewery in America was run by John Wagner of Philadelpia, a city with a large population of German immigrants.

German tavern-breweries quickly grew into large urban breweries with a production capacity of several thousands of barrels per year, a far cry from the 18th century colonial tavern-breweries of the 18th century. By 1860, lager breweries were producing more beer than ale breweries.

Several well-known breweries which survived into the 20th century got their start in this first wave of German immigrant breweries: Joseph Schlitz bought a small brewery in a restaurant in 1856; Valentin Blatz bought a brewery in 1851; Frederick Miller acquired the Plank Road Brewery in 1855 — all in Milwaukee.

In St. Louis, Eberhard Anheuser, a soap manufacturer, found himself the owner of a small brewery started by a man named Schneider. Anheuser brought his son-in-law, Adolphus Busch, a brewer supplier, into the business creating what was to become the most famous and successful brewery in American history.

WESTWARD EXPANSION

Brewing also followed the westward expansion of America. The first breweries opened in Oregon and California as soon as settlers arrived. Henry Weinhard bought a small brewery in Portland and began selling to saloons throughout the Northwest in 1859.

San Francisco had no shortage of breweries after the 1849 Gold Rush. In 1852, the city boasted 350 barrooms and similar establishments where beer was sold. There were reportedly 15 breweries in San Francisco by 1856, most owned by Germans.

Wherever gold prospecters rushed, breweries were not far behind; Sacramento had its first brewery in 1849, followed by breweries in Eureka, Yuba City, Nicholaus, Marysville, Stockton, and El Dorado.

Many California breweries made steam beer, a lager beer not stored at cold temperatures. The "steam" probably referred to extra carbonation after the beer had been "krausened" (primed with unfermented malt before storage). The additional carbonation would "steam" out of the warm, wooden casks when opened, much like steam released from a boiling kettle.

San Francisco remained a center for brewing in California while inland areas began growing grapes for wine making. Hops and barley were grown in fertile areas; the small town of Hopland, 90 miles north of San Francisco in Mendocino County, became well-known for growing hops.

THE CIVIL WAR AND THE FIRST TAX ON BEER

The decade before the Civil War was a time of growth for American breweries. In 1850 there were 431 breweries producing 750,000 barrels of beer; in 1860, there were 1,269 breweries producing a million barrels of beer in the U.S. New York and Philadephia were still brewing centers, making 85% of the beer. Breweries were also expanding in cities all over the country — St. Paul, Chicago, Boston, Albany, Baltimore and Cincinnati.

At the beginning of the Civil War, breweries were happily filling orders for troops on both sides of the Mason-Dixon Line. But the greatest contribution breweries made to the bloody war was not to quench the troops' thirst, but to pay for the war. In 1862, Congress enacted the Internal Revenue Act which levied a $1 tax on every barrel of beer and required a license for each brewery.

The 1862 Internal Revenue Tax also made the brewers — who were becoming wealthy manufacturers — realize they needed to organize. That same year a group of predominantly lager brewers gathered in New York. They agreed to meet annually and in 1864 named themselves the United States Brewers Association. Their reason for organizing was to fight the tax, and they were successful in reducing it temporarily to 60 cents per barrel.

The association consisted mostly of lager brewers, which meant German immigrants. The proceedings for the first meetings were in German; it was not until 1875 that English became the official language of the association.

The tax proved to be a boon to the industry. It rallied to present one voice to the government and began studying better managment practices at the brewery. The industry was united with lobbyists in Washington and a national organization to represent it. Brewing was also becoming a major industry in America; by 1867, there were breweries in every state, and production from the nation's 3,700 brewers reached 6 million barrels per year.

THE REVIVAL OF THE PROHIBITION MOVEMENT

As soon as the brewers' association had taken care of their tax situation in Washington, they turned their attention to a problem that was to prove more threatening than the Internal Revenue Tax — prohibition.

The temperance movement had declined in the 1850s and through the Civil War. But after the war, prohibitionists were again making noises. The first Presidential campaign in which prohibition was an issue was in 1872. Horace Greeley, editor of the *New York Tribune,* was an outspoken prohibitionist who aroused the considerable anti-German sentiment in the country. General Grant ran for a second term on a Republican Party platform with a mild statment on temperance.

Despite the growing sentiment toward prohibition, the brewers argued that their industry was important for the national economy. They claimed that in 1873, 55% of all taxes collected by the Internal Revenue Tax came from brewers and distillers. That year, the number of American breweries reached 4,131, the highest ever attained.

THE GOLDEN AGE OF AMERICAN BREWING

American breweries came of age at the 1876 Centennial Exhibition in Philadelphia. The industry built a two-story exhibit hall and displayed the latest technology in making beer. To show how far brewing had advanced since the American Revolution, they set up a small colonial tavern to demonstrate how early brewing was done by hand.

To answer the prohibitionists, at the Centennial Exhibition the brewers issued a pamphlet, "Essays on the Malt Liquor Question," which said, "That a brewer is just as necessary to the commonweal as a butcher, a baker, a tailor, a builder, or any other economic industry, is proven by the present position of the trade in the United States."

Extravagant expositions provided brewers with a showcase to laud their achievements. This was the heyday of splashy, opulent exhibitions such as the 1878 Paris Exposition, the World's Exposition in 1884-85, Chicago's 1893 Fair, and the Lewis and Clark Centennial Exposition in 1905. American breweries prominently displayed in the expositions and medals were handed out to the beers which competed in elaborate tastings.

The 1905 Louisiana Purchase Exposition in St. Louis was the largest in the U.S. up to that time. Adolphus Busch was a major backer and saw to it that the achievements of the German people in America were sufficiently recognized. For his effort, the Kaiser awarded Busch the Order of the Crown, second class, in 1905.

A MODERN INDUSTRY

The Golden Age of Brewing was a time of great change in the manufacturing, distributing, and marketing of beer. From the 1850s until Prohibition (1920), the American brewing industry evolved from a struggling collection of infant breweries into a united, highly mechanical, national industry with a powerful lobby in Washington.

Another change that had taken place in brewing in the 50 years was the type of beer that Americans were choosing to drink. While ale (as well as porter and stout) had been the most popular drink in the 1600s and 1700s, lager became the choice of more Americans in the 1800s.

Americans had even selected the lighter, carbonated pilsner lager over other lager beers to drink year around. The influence of the temperance movement cannot be overlooked in the shift to the lower alcohol pilsner.

Science was also playing a larger role in the brewing process. Although Louis Pasteur is better known today for the process of providing uncontaminated milk, he did most of his work studying fermentation in beer. His classic work "Etudes sur la Biere," or "The Study of Beer," determined the role of yeast in fermentation.

Danish chemists isolated two principal brewing yeasts, *Saccharomyces cerevisiae* (top-fermenting ale yeast) and *Saccharomyces carlsbergensis* (bottom-fermenting or lager yeast). In 1883, Danish chemist Emil Hansen introduced to the Carlsberg Brewery the first pure lager yeast propagated from a single cell. From this came the first strain of yeast free from wild yeasts or bacteria which impart undesirable taste in beer.

The Pabst Brewery in Milwaukee brewed with the first pure lager yeast in 1887 and was the first American brewery to hire a chemist for brewing.

One obstacle brewers had to mass marketing their beer was putting a reliable stopper on the bottle tops. Corks had been used widely, but were expensive, not always reliable and required hand application. Varieties of metal crown tops had been tried, but proved difficult to manufacture because bottle tops were not uniform in size and dimension. Once commercial glass making was able to produce uniform bottle sizes, crown tops could be manufactured to fit them.

The advent of a national railroad network (and refrigerated rail-cars) was a major boon to national breweries. They could ship beer cross-country and compete more aggressively with small breweries. National brewers became fierce competitors using expensive advertising and superior facilities to attract new customers.

BREWERY MERGERS

Brewing became a major industry while America was evolving from an agrarian society into a world industrial power. In 1850, there were 421 commercial breweries in America; by 1860, the number had almost tripled.

From 1880 to 1910, the production of beer was increasing while the number of breweries was declining (1,500 in 1910 which produced 59½ million barrels). Most of these were local breweries serving a neighborhood or small town with deliveries by horse-drawn wagons.

The late 19th century saw the advent of the truly national brewers; Pabst and Schlitz of Milwaukee and Anheuser-Busch of St. Louis reached this level at the turn of the century when their capacity reached 1 million barrels per year.

But another trend was taking place at the turn of the century that had more of an impact on the evolution of brewing than showy expositions. That was the wave of mergers and consolidations that became a stampede. Virtually every major city experienced this merger trend; in Pittsburgh, 21 brewers consolidated into the Pittsburgh Brewing Company in 1899. In 1905, 15 other Pittsburgh brewers joined to become the Independent Brewing Company.

A trade publication, "The Western Brewer," called the trend "an almost insane craze." The aim of mergers, of course, was competition. And when the price wars began, only the larger, national brewers could survive. The larger breweries also bought corner saloons, beer gardens, taverns, restaurants and even hotels to expand their retail outlets.

Pabst at one time owned nine hotels and restaurants in New York, Chicago, Minneapolis, San Francisco and Milwaukee. Anheuser-Busch owned the Adolphus Hotel in Dallas and interest in two St. Louis restaurants.

Although "corner saloons" were profitable outlets for breweries, they proved detrimental in the pre-Prohibition rallies when impassioned speakers called them "dens of evil."

PROHIBITION BECOMES NATIONAL ISSUE

By the turn of the century, prohibition was becoming an issue in national elections and all presidential candidates were forced to take a position on the volatile issue. Theodore Roosevelt wrote to Republican candidate William Taft about prohibitionists, "If ever there was a wicked attitude it is that of those fantastic extremists who advocate a law so drastic that it cannot be enforced, knowing perfectly well that lawlessness and contempt of the law follow, . . . My experience with prohibitionists, however, is that the best way to deal with them is to ignore them."

The move for a national prohibition law was launched in 1913 with a dramatic parade on Washington calling for a constitutional amendment. A House vote in 1914 was 197 for, 190 against, a majority but not enough for the two-thirds required under the Constitution.

By 1916, 23 states had passed "dry" laws; a war of propaganda was raging throughout the country. The brewers, however, were never effective in organizing a mass movement to counter the shrill rhetoric of the prohibitionists.

The declaration of war against Germany in 1917 coincided with passage of a Food Control Bill ending the distilling of spirits. President Wilson, however, had the authority to permit the brewing of beer with an alcohol content of 2¾% by weight.

Prohibition was not hindered by the anti-German sentiment rampant during World War I. The Anti-Saloon League wasted no time portraying German brewers as subversive to the war effort and a Senate investigation looked into ties between brewers of German ancestry and the Allied Powers.

PROHIBITION

The 18th Amendment calling for prohibition was ratified by the required 36 states on January 16, 1919. In May 1919, Representative Volstead of Minnesota introduced a bill establishing the apparatus for enforcing prohibition. Congress passed the bill in October; President Wilson vetoed the bill, but Congress overrode it hastily. Prohibition was to begin one year from the date of ratification, January 16, 1920.

The success of the prohibitionists was partially aided by the overall poor public relations of the brewers and their failure to organize any group of citizens to represent their views. Presented with prohibition, brewers were forced to close their doors or switch to manufacturing non-alcoholic products: vinegar, near-beer (½ of 1% alcohol), malt extract, fruit juices, breakfast food or commercial feed. An article in the "American Brewer" said, "Brewers who entered the field of cereal, beverages or soft drink manufacture were disappointed by the poor demand for their product."

Anheuser-Busch manufactured household products; Schlitz made chocolate and candy; Blatz produced industrial alcohol; Fortune Brothers Brewing of Chicago manufactured spaghetti and macaroni; Stevenson Brewing of New York used part of their plant to store furs. Most breweries, however, were forced to shut their doors — many forever.

Enforcing prohibition proved to be impossible, regardless of how much money or how many people the Federal Prohibition Commission could muster. The national response to prohibition was speakeasies, bathtub gin, illegal stills and gang warfare. Prohibition fed corruption, since the majority was not sympathetic to the intent of the Volstead Act. The issue was never put before a national referendum but was forced through state legislatures. It was 1930 and the beginning of the Depression before a nationwide movement emerged to repeal the Volstead Act.

A wave of defections from the ranks of the prohibitionists, including John D. Rockefeller, led to a stampede for repeal at the 1932 national political conventions. Franklin Roosevelt campaigned on a repeal platform and shortly after his election, hearings were begun in the House to modify the Volstead Act. Congressman Fiorello La Guardia testified in support of repeal, " . . . first, by reason of the great need of additional revenue; second, owing to the complete failure of prohibition enforcement; third, by reason of the changed attitude on the part of the American public."

Jobs in breweries turned out to be a persuasive argument in favor of repeal: coopers, bottlers, maltsters, hop-growers, truck drivers and warehouse hands were a large segment of the unemployed in the 1930s.

REPEAL OF PROHIBITION

Shortly after Roosevelt was sworn into office, he sent a message to Congress on March 13, 1933, seeking "modification of the Volstead Act." The repeal legislation that passed also enacted a $5 tax per barrel and a tax of $1,000 per brewery.

The first 3.2% beer since 1920 became legal on April 7, 1933, in the 19 states that did not have prohibition laws on their books. America held the first legal "beer" party in 13 years, and the celebrating went on for days.

Repeal did not solve all problems for the breweries; it was a new world and many of the old ways had long since disappeared. A once-powerful industry capable of sponsoring international expositions was reduced to a few companies producing everything from ice cream and soft drinks to vinegar, cooking supplies and candy.

By June 1933, 31 breweries were back in business; a year later, there were 756, the most that ever emerged after Prohibition. But times were far from rosy for the breweries; the nation was in the midst of a devastating Depression and high unemployment. Brewers sought a reduction in the $5 per barrel tax in order to sell beer at 5 cents a glass. In 1933, only 20½ million barrels of beer were brewed, far below the pre-prohibition figure of 60 million barrels per year. Soft drinks had also captured a share of the market. Plus, a new round of federal and state regulations came with repeal that put restrictions on all aspects of brewing, distributing and marketing beer.

TECHNOLOGY AND WORLD WAR II LEAD TO MAJOR CHANGES IN BREWING

The introduction of the metal can made significant changes in the drinking habits of the country. Once most beer drinking was confined to taverns or saloons. But when the Krueger Brewing Company of Newark became the first brewery to put its beer in cans on January 24, 1935, it revolutionized beer packaging. Draught beer dispensed in mugs or buckets was no longer the only alternative for home consumption. Soon, every brewery was canning its beer; changes in commercial glassmaking also made bottled beer more available.

Brewery advertising quickly adapted and featured family members enjoying beer at home, sitting by the radio, swimming, playing tennis — but *not* at the local saloon. By 1940, beer consumption had reached pre-prohibition levels although there were only half the breweries operating.

In 1940, six breweries (Anheuser-Busch, Schlitz, Pabst, Ballantine, Schaefer and Ruppert) were selling 1 million barrels per year. Although more than 700 breweries opened after Repeal, by 1940, there were only 52 large enough to produce a quarter-million barrels a year.

With the looming war, brewers were frightened that prohibition again would be visited upon them like it had been in the early days of America's involvement in World War I. The attitude in the country, however, had little interest in repeating the excesses and corruption of Prohibition. Chief of Staff General George C. Marshall, in commenting about allowing beer to be served on military bases, said, "It would be harmful to the men in the service to direct a prohibition against them that did not apply to other citizens. To do so would inevitably lead to intemperance."

Beer actually contributed to the morale of men in uniform and the government required brewers to set aside a portion of their 3.2% beer for the military. Key brewery workers were granted deferments at the discretion of local draft boards and women worked in breweries when there were shortages of men.

Beer sales soared during World War II from 53 million barrels in 1940 to 80 million barrels in 1945, the most ever recorded. But breweries were also producing thinner, lighter beers using corn and rice adjuncts in response to the governmental rationing of barley.

INDUSTRIAL BREWERIES

Breweries did not suffer like other industries that made drastic changes to meet the demands of wartime production. Breweries essentially stayed the same and by the end of the war, were prospering. Most were old breweries that traced their beginnings to the 19th century and had operated in facilities built 60 or 70 years ago.

But the greatest changes going on in the industry after World War II were not in brewing; they were in packaging, distributing, advertising and marketing. The breweries capable of making the changes were the million-barrel-per-year industrial giants who could market and advertise across the country as well as they could across the street.

The predominant trend in brewing in the 1950s and '60s was to expand production and increase markets. This was accomplished best by the largest breweries — Anheuser-Busch, Pabst, Schlitz, and Falstaff. Soon these breweries were buying small breweries to increase production at subsidiary plants. The Falstaff brewery in St. Louis bought breweries in Omaha and New Orleans; Schlitz bought a brewery in Brooklyn. Anheuser-Busch countered by building a new brewery in Newark in 1951 and another in Los Angeles that cost $20 million.

California was becoming a booming beer market and soon most industrial breweries — Falstaff, Anheuser-Busch, Hamm's, Schlitz, and Pabst had plants on the West Coast. Florida was another big market, with the dramatic increase in population following World War II.

A "shakedown" was coming; there were simply too many breweries selling beer in the same markets. Pabst absorbed Blatz; Narragansett bought Kreuger; Miller bought Gettleman.

From the 1950s through the 1980s, a massive concentration was going on in the brewing industry. While the number of breweries was shrinking to fewer than 50 by the mid-1970s, the market share was dominated by just a few breweries. By 1985, the two largest breweries, Anheuser-Busch (68 million barrels) and Miller (37 million barrels) were responsible for 63% of domestic beer production and the top five breweries (Anheuser-Busch, Miller, Stroh, Heileman and Coors) controlled 94% of the domestic beer market.

FIRST MICROBREWERIES APPEAR

It was against this domination by massive industrial breweries with plants located in the largest beer markets (California, Texas, New York) that the first tiny microbreweries began appearing in the late 1970s on the West Coast. The microbrewers had no hopes of challenging the industrial breweries at marketing or production; rather, they had only one feature to offer: creativity in brewing specialty beers. With money, hard work and some luck, this creativity could find a market in the growing number of consumers who wanted more than "industrial-brewed" light lager that had dominated the marketplace since the end of World War II.

Whether Jack McAuliffe realized it in the summer of 1977 when he was brewing a few test batches of New Albion Ale in Sonoma, he was about to begin a new era — small breweries soon to be scattered all over the country that harkened back to an earlier time when brewing was a "cottage industry" and the choice in beers was diverse and rich.

With New Albion, Boulder, Cartwright, Sierra Nevada, Newmans and the other early microbreweries, brewing in America had come full circle. Once again, brewing was done in small batches by artisans who took their craft seriously. Furthermore, their beer was sold around the community where the people who drank it could actually say they knew their brewer.

It had been a long time since brewing was done that way in America.

★　　★　　★

— *4* —

THE CAMPAIGN FOR REAL ALE (CAMRA)

Americans learned about microbrewing from the same people who taught us about justice, bicameral legislatures, fashion, rock music and reverence for royal families.

In many ways, American microbrewers are duplicating what a band of intrepid English ale lovers set out to do in the 1970s — bring back some cherished brewing customs that were in great danger of disappearing forever. Many early microbrewers (including Bill Newman, Newmans; Mike Hale, Hale's Ales) even worked in English breweries to learn the craft of small-scale brewing.

BIG SIX BREWING MONOPOLY

Twenty years ago, the "Big Six" breweries in England (Watney Mann & Truman, Whitbread, Scottish & Newcastle, Bass, Courage, Allied) had all but monopolized brewing and selling beer in England, a trend being duplicated in America at the same time. But the Big Six industrial breweries were making far-reaching changes without the support of millions of their countrymen who considered themselves lovers of traditional ale.

English law allows breweries to have "tied houses" or pubs that serve as retail outlets. Before Prohibition, American breweries also had tied house corner saloons selling their beer. In the '50s and '60s, the Big Six went on a rampage, gobbling up small breweries and pubs which had been around for many years. At one time, Bass owned almost 9,000 pubs; Whitbread more than 7,000.

Buying pubs was legal, but the Big Six were seen as threatening a way of life that most patriotic Englishmen cherished as their birthright. The neighborhood pub, after all, was as much a part of English life as the *Times,* afternoon tea and tweeds.

The Big Six also were brewing lager, which offended the taste buds of most English drinkers used to a rich selection of ales, porters and stouts traditionally found in pubs. To meet markets all over the British Isles, the Big Six kegged (and pasteurized and carbonated) their lager, a departure from the cask-conditioned ales pubs had dispensed for centuries.

REAL ALE

Cask conditioned ales are fresh beer containing live yeast in the casks, which produces a secondary fermentation and live "real ale" when served. Keg beer, on the other hand, is inert — a sterile beverage that can be stored for months or shipped long distances. The difference between cask-conditioned ale and kegged lager was enough to start a peaceful rebellion by real ale traditionalists around England.

But traditional ale wasn't all "real alers" were fighting for; they also wanted to preserve neighborhood pubs which the Big Six brewers were converting into theme pubs, discos and American-style fern bars. The horror that English traditionalists foresaw was chains of identical pizza pubs and their like serving bland, heavily carbonated and kegged lager beer. Civil wars have been fought for less.

If the Big Six brewers succeeded, gone forever would be quaint village pubs with charming names like Dog & Pheasant, George & Dragon, Struggling Monkey, Royal Fusiler, and Merrie Monk. The threat posed by the industrial breweries to neighborhood pubs was too great; a consumer rebellion was brewing.

In 1971, four Englishmen on holiday met in an Irish pub and lamented the trend toward industrialized beer and chain pubs. When they returned home, they began organizing patriotic ale lovers, pub crawlers, social historians, traditionalists, eccentric philosophers, and neighbor-hood conservationists. The result was The Campaign for Real Ale or CAMRA.

The movement grew rapidly and captured the imagination of the media and the public. CAMRA prepared a series of reports on the monopolization of the big brewers, organized beer festivals around the country and sponsored an annual week-long national beer festival.

Along the way, CAMRA educated both public and Parliament about the threat posed by the Big Six. As awareness about CAMRA and its goals grew, small victories turned into major triumphs. Some industrial brewers gave into the demand for real ale and began brewing it again. The government ruled that pubs had to post a price list of all beers served, something the big brewers had been fighting for years. A report was presented to Parliament on the Big Six monopoly.

CAMRA today is a thriving organization of 25,000 real ale lovers organized into 150 regional groups in England, Scotland and Wales. The claim has even been made that CAMRA is "the world's most suc-cessful consumer organization," having revived a way of life — real ale and authentic English pubs — that was rapidly on its way to extinction.

CAMRA GOOD BEER GUIDE

CAMRA today has a small staff that operates out of a crowded townhouse in the industrial town of St. Albans (34 Alma Road, St. Albans, Hertfordshire, AL1 3BR U.K.) and publishes a charming and highly informative annual "Good Beer Guide," that contains the names of 5,000 pubs that carry real ale in an authentic pub atmosphere (Eng-land has 66,000 pubs!). According to CAMRA, "The quality of the beer is the overriding consideration for inclusion in the Guide: each pub must sell consistently good draught beer for at least six months before it is considered for selection."

In addition to featuring real ale pubs, the "Good Beer Guide" lists about 200 independent breweries (such as Alexandra, Ballards, But-combe, Guernsey, Hydes, Mendip United, Raven, Samuel Smith) and about 70 homebrew pubs (Alford Arms, Battersea, Beer Engine, Fleece & Firkin, Frog & Parrot, Hall Cross, Lass o'Gowrie, Long Barn, Three Tuns). CAMRA maps show thirsty pub-crawlers their way around England via routes that take them to the most memorable pubs. Re-gional CAMRA groups publish guides to local pubs.

CAMRA awards an annual "Pub of the Year" in two categories, best refurbishing and best new pub. In 1985, the Britannia Inn, Oswaldtwistle, Lancashire and the Bricklayer's Arms, Gresse Street, London, won best refurbishment. No pub was selected for best new pub.

LICENSING LAWS

CAMRA's latest challenge — more ambitious than taking on the Big Six — is to modify England's licensing laws that restrict pubs to 9½ hours per day all over the country. Most pubs open around 10:00 AM until about 2:30 PM, then must close until late afternoon. With a few exceptions, pubs all over England must close at 11:00 PM and are not open on Sundays.

Originally legislated in 1915 to restrict steel workers from spending too much time in pubs during World War I, the licensing laws remained on the books far longer than intended. Most Englishmen and women consider licensing laws more than just petty and restrictive; they regard them as offensive to their character and heritage. CAMRA already claims credit for making progress in Scotland, Ireland and the Channel Islands where pub hours are now more liberal.

CAMRA also protests the bite the British government takes out of each pint of ale. "Beer in Britain is taxed more heavily than in any other EEC (European Economic Community) country except the Irish Republic," the *Good Beer Guide* claims.

The Guide follows similar movements in the U.S. Canada, New Zealand, Australia, Germany and Belgium, and presents an annual "state of the ale" message about brewing around the world. The book sells for a modest 4.50 pounds (or about $7 U.S.) and is seen in pubs throughout Britain.

Pubs selected to appear in the Guide wear their honor proudly, often displaying CAMRA mirrors, towels or banners to let customers know they are purveyors of real ale and not the foamy, ersatz beer produced by the Big Six mega-keggeries.

WHEN IN ENGLAND . . .

Anyone visiting England should track down a copy of the latest CAMRA *Good Beer Guide* and locate a couple pubs listed in the guide. Over a pint or two of cask-conditioned ale, one can soak up some authentic pub atmosphere and maybe hear the publican tell "war stories" about CAMRA and the pub revival movement.

The Tower of London and Westminster Abbey are historic landmarks that no tourist to England should miss. But a few hours spent in a classic English pub can be just as educational as visiting the well-known tourist haunts. You're also likely to develop an appreciation for real ale and understand why thousands joined CAMRA to preserve a way of life that is just as cherished in England as the royal family.

★ ★ ★

— *5* —

STYLES OF
MICROBREWED BEER

One of the greatest contributions microbreweries have made is reintroducing classic beer styles that had all but disappeared in America when the industrial breweries began dictating the one style of beer Americans would drink — light lager.

In addition to brewing excellent lagers (using more barley and hops per barrel than industrial breweries), American microbreweries are also brewing ales, seasonal beers, bocks, porters, stouts and wheat beers. These beers are still being brewed in England, Belgium and Germany and were brewed in America before Prohibition.

Beer is not just light lager; there are a hundred different beers depending upon the creativity of the brewer and the quality of ingredients. The comparison is often made between bread and beer. At one time, "white bread" was virtually the only kind that could be found in supermarkets. Today, however, one can find a rich variety of special breads baked by smaller bakeries — rye, sourdough, pumpernickel, whole wheat, raisin, egg, French, Italian, Afghan and pita. The same choice once faced the American beer consumer when he or she ventured to the liquor store or supermarket — cases of industrial-brewed beer that was virtually the same light lager: Budweiser, Stroh, Miller, Coors,

Pabst and Schlitz. Microbreweries now offer a diversity that includes light and dark ales, porters, amber lagers, wheat beer, bocks and seasonal beers.

For those who have not tried microbrewed beer, a world of new flavors and styles awaits them. Many supermarkets and liquor stores even allow customers to buy single beers instead of a six-pack of the same beer. That means customers can walk out with six different microbrewed beers to sample instead of drinking six identical beers.

What microbrewering offers is choice: a choice in taste, flavors and styles of beers that once was restricted to travelers to Europe. It's a refreshing change and one that promises to get even more diverse in the years to come.

Enjoy!

All beers fall into two categories, lagers or ales, depending upon the brewing process and the yeast used. The following are the types of beer brewed by North American microbreweries.

LAGERS

Lagers are brewed with *Saccharomyces carlsbergensis,* a yeast which settles to the bottom when it has finished fermenting and which ferments at low temperatures, usually 45-55 degrees Fahrenheit. Lager comes from the German word *lagern,* "to store"; lagers traditionally are stored and chilled for three or four weeks.

The longer storage time required for lager (as well as the additional storage tanks) translates into increased capital and space — scarce commodities for most microbreweries. That is why the first microbreweries (started by homebrewers) usually brewed ales because of the shorter brewing time. They couldn't wait three or four weeks to sell their beer.

Pilsners — a general term for beer brewed with hard, acid water. Since Prohibition, most breweries in America have brewed this light lager, but with a mild, hoppy taste. To many, pilsners are the least objectionable style of beer since they are relatively mild and not astringent.

Pilsner refers to the Bohemian town of Pilsen, Czechoslovakia, where hops were grown for centuries. The classic Pilsner Urquell beer is still brewed in Pilsen.

Light beer — lager with dextrin eliminated to lower calories (85-95 calories per bottle). Major American brewers have successfully marketed the concept of "lite" beer, but microbreweries have avoided the stampede since their uniqueness is to brew authentic beers and not be faddish. Some breweries use industrial enzymes to lighten their beer; others simply add water at the end of the brewing cycle. Any enterprising beer drinker could do the same with carbonated water and avoid the fuss.

Boulder began brewing their Sport beer in February 1987, promoting it as a light beer to compete with the popular Mexican and Canadian imports.

Bock — German for strong beer; usually a dark colored beer served in the spring or autumn. Bock beer originally came from Einbeck, from which its name was derived. The beer even has its own mascot, the billygoat (bock means goat in German) which adorns most bock labels.

There are several types of bock beers such as Maibock (May beer) or Doppelbock (double bock), but only a few are brewed in America (Kessler, Hibernia, Widmer). Bock is brewed with more malt to yield a stronger beer. The dark roasted malts frequently used in bock beers give them a sweeter flavor and darker color.

Malt liquor — a term sometimes used for beer that is 5% or more alcohol. Not really a liquor (actually just a pale lager), but some state laws require the name to indicate the higher alcohol content. Some states such as California require microbreweries (Sierra Nevada, St. Stanislaus) to use the term "malt liquor" on their labels because their beer has a higher alcohol content.

Steam beer — once a popular beer in California, the name probably came from the extra carbonation from brewing in warm temperatures. The category refers to a bottom-fermented beer (like a lager) but fermented at higher temperature (like an ale). The result is a beer that combines both characteristics of lager and an ale.

Before refrigeration, steam beer would have been an alternative to brewing lager beer when the colder lagering temperatures (32-35 degrees Fahrenheit) would have been impossible to achieve during the summer months in California. The term could refer to the violent release of carbonation "steam" when the warm casks were tapped in the California summers.

Anchor Brewing in San Francisco has copyrighted the name steam beer and brews their beer in shallow, open vats during the first stage of fermentation. The original Anchor brewery also brewed steam beer.

Weiss beer — typically a German style beer (brewed with top fermenting yeast) made with wheat in addition to barley malt for lighter (or white) color. The amount of wheat may vary from 10% up to 60% depending upon the style and taste desired.

Wheat beers can be pale-colored and taste tangy and spicy, or may be darker and heavier like the Dunkel Weizen beers (*weisse* means "white" in German; *weizen* means "wheat"). Several American microbreweries (including Anchor, Hart, Kessler, Yakima and Hibernia) brew wheat beers. They are a summertime drink served with a twist of lemon.

Vienna — a reddish or copper-colored lager originally brewed in Vienna. Similar to Marzenbier (March beer), laid down in caves in the spring to be drunk in the fall.

ALES

Ales, generally English and Irish styles, are top fermenting beers, which means the ale yeast *(Saccharomyces cerevisae)* rises to the top of the vessel and ferments at higher temperatures (60-70 degrees F). Ales can be any color from light amber to reddish, to brown and even black. Their tastes can range from slightly bitter and thin to heavy and sweet (depending upon the amount and type of hops used). Most ales have a fruitiness characteristic of warm fermentation.

Altbier — an early German beer style (*alt* means old in German) before lagers became popular in the 19th century. Alt was brewed like an ale at higher temperature and is still brewed in Dusseldorf and Cologne.

Alt is brewed with an ale yeast, but stored (lagered) at cold temperature for a few weeks. It is usually dark or copper colored, well-hopped and resembles a British ale. The Widmer and St. Stanislaus microbreweries brew alt beers.

Barley wine — actually an ale, but called a wine because of the higher alcohol content. Sierra Nevada brews small quantities of the popular Bigfoot Barleywine, the strongest beer brewed in America (8-9% alcohol). Anchor also brews Foghorn barley wine.

Bitter — an English style of beer that is highly hopped; the taste is not really "bitter," just tangy.

Pale ale — a copper-colored bottled ale which is the equivalent of the British draft bitters. There are many types of pale ales brewed by microbreweries (Hales, Anchor, Sierra Nevada, Newmans, Independent, Pyramid, Yakima, Spinnakers). They can vary greatly from light to dark; sweet to bitter.

Porter — British-style ale made with darker malt; slightly bittersweet with chocolate-like flavor. The name refers to the porters in 18th century England who drank a combination of ale and stout (called 'alf 'n' 'alf) poured together. Several North American microbreweries brew porter (Anchor, Sierra Nevada, Spinnakers).

Stout — very dark, almost black ale made with roasted malt. English stouts can be sweet (Mackeson) or dry (Guinness); Yakima Brewing makes a classic Russian-style Imperial Stout which includes honey to create a potent (7% alcohol), heavy-bodied, bittersweet beer.

★   ★   ★

— *6* —

HOW BEER IS BREWED

Beer originally consisted of only four ingredients: barley, hops, yeast and water.

But now, all major breweries use other cereal grains such as wheat, rice or corn to make thinner, lighter beers. Grains other than barley are called "adjuncts," which are usually shunned by microbreweries. A few microbreweries use wheat as an adjunct to brew wheat beer in the summer.

MALTING

Barley is a cereal grain similar in appearance to wheat. After the barley has been harvested, it is taken to a malthouse where it is soaked in water. The barley germinates, producing enzymes which can convert starch into fermentable sugar.

After germination, water is drained and the barley is heated in a kiln to stop germination. The temperature at which the barley is heated will determine the type of malt that results.

Malt heated at lower temperatures will be pale malt. A higher temperature will result in darker malt such as that are used in amber and copper-colored ales. If the malt is heated to high temperatures, the grain will be roasted and become dark. Roasted malt is black and is used for brewing dark lagers, porters, and stouts.

MASHING

The malted barley is milled or crushed into a coarse powder called grist. The grist is poured into a "mash tun" vessel and hot water is added. This hot, thick mash sits for several hours and becomes rich in malt enzymes which reduce insoluble starch to fermentable sugars.

The sugary solution is drained from the mash tun and the mash is washed with more hot water to remove sugars still trapped within the grains. This process is called "sparging."

The sweet liquid removed from the mash tun is now called "wort" (pronounced "wert"), which is run into a copper or stainless steel brewkettle where it is boiled for several hours. During the rolling boil, hops are added. Hops (extract, whole or pelletized) added early in the boil are for bitterness (bittering hops); hops added at the end of the boil are for aroma (finishing hops).

FERMENTATION

After hops are removed from the brewkettle, the hot wort is sent to fermenting vessels which can be closed or open. Yeast is added or "pitched" into the wort and fermentation begins. Yeast ferments sugars in the wort into alcohol (ethanol) and carbon dioxide. During the initial process of fermentation, the yeast propagates rapidly, producing carbon dioxide and foam on top of the fermenting vessel. Approximately five days after the yeast has been pitched, initial fermentation is over; the "green beer" that remains is 60-80% fermented.

Ales, which are fermented at warmer temperatures (60-75 degrees F), may be primed with additional sugar. A secondary fermentation takes place for lager beers at temperatures down to 32 degrees F. Some breweries add a small amount of unfermented wort during the secondary fermentation. This process is called "krausening" and gives the beer smoothness and more even carbonation. Krausened beer contains smaller bubbles which produce more foam and a richer head when poured.

Lagering can be for a few days, weeks, or even months for strong seasonal beers like bock and Christmas beers. This slower, colder fermentation produces a clearer, crisper beer typical of lager.

PASTEURIZATION

The final product, lager or ale, may be filtered or pasteurized depending upon the brewer's choice. Pasteurization stabilizes beer, but many claim the heat destroys a beer's fine hop aroma.

Many microbrewers choose cold filtering over pasteurization to avoid tampering with the delicate hopping effect they are trying to achieve.

(There are many technical books on the brewing process. For anyone interested in homebrewing, several references in the bibliography are excellent places to learn about this hobby. Anyone considering homebrewing, however, should keep in mind that many adventurous homebrewers unknowingly took their first step to becoming microbrewers when they brewed their first batch of homebrew. Readers are cautioned that a pleasant weekend home brewing hobby can turn into a commercial microbrewing undertaking unless one is able to control his ambitions and dreams. See Mares' "Making Beer"; Noonan's "Brewing Lager Beer"; and Papazian's "Complete Joy of Homebrewing.")

A DIRECTORY OF AMERICAN MICROBREWERIES

(Production figures are based on preliminary information gathered early in 1987 by the American Homebrewers Association and *Brewers Digest*. Figures for microbreweries that opened in 1986 were not complete due to limited production. When there was an inconsistency, 1985 production figures compiled by *Modern Brewery Age* were used.)

CALIFORNIA

ANCHOR BREWING COMPANY
1705 Mariposa Street
San Francisco, California 94107
 (415) 863-8350

President/Brewmaster: Fritz Maytag
Founded: 1965
1985 Production: 38,000 barrels

Fritz Maytag was studying Japanese at Stanford University in the early 1960s when he heard San Francisco's Anchor brewery was about to close. The Maytag heir visited the old brewery and fell in love with it; he soon became the owner and the rest, as they say, is history.

Maytag became intimately involved in all aspects of brewing and dedicated himself to restoring Anchor to the prominence it had once held as a brewery of "steam beer," a California product with a history going back to the Gold Rush days.

Almost single-handedly, Maytag turned Anchor into the flagship of small breweries (the term "microbreweries" hadn't even been created yet). He learned how to brew "steam beer" (and copyrighted the term), designed new packaging and came up with a marketing plan that established Anchor as a premier American beer.

One of Maytag's greatest contributions as a brewer has been reviving beer styles that had almost disappeared in America — porter, wheat, stout, steam and seasonal ales. More than half of the microbreweries in America now produce more than one beer style (some as many as three).

Anchor Steam — *the official trademark of Anchor; brewed with American two-row malting barley and several varieties of hops.*

Liberty Ale — *originally a Christmas Ale which became so popular that Anchor now brews it regularly.*

Anchor Porter

Anchor's Christmas Ale — *since 1975, Anchor brews a special beer for the holiday season with a new label every year.*

Anchor Wheat — *contains more than 60% wheat malt.*

Old Foghorn — *a barley wine.*

PALO ALTO BREWING COMPANY
240 B Polaris Avenue
Mountain View, California 94043
    (415) 965-9660

President: Bob Stoddard
Brewmaster: Ray Brewer
Founded: 1983
1985 Production: 1,500 barrels

Palo Alto originally packaged their ale in attractive liter bottles and 1 gallon kegs in a box (the equivalent of a 12 pack). Their prime marketing area is Santa Clara and San Mateo Counties in the south Bay area.

Palo Alto uses malt extract in brewing.

London Real Ale —*brewed with two-row malt and two English hops, Fuggles and E. Kent Goldings.*

★   ★   ★

PASADENA BREWING COMPANY
28 East Colorado Boulevard
Pasadena, California 91105
   (818) 796-8090

President: Edward S. Odjana
Founded: 1986

By selling its first beer at the end of December, Pasadena Brewing became the last of some 15 new microbreweries that opened in America in 1986. Founder Ed Odjana was a former Rand analyst, UCLA instructor and head of corporate planning at Olympia before he came up with the idea to start a microbrewery in Los Angeles.

Although there are many microbreweries that begin via contract brewing, Pasadena has the distinction of being part of the first international contract brewing arrangement between the U.S. and Canada. The California brewery is having its beer brewed at the Granville Island microbrewery in Vancouver and delivered by refrigerated truck to Pasadena.

Odjana rushed through the brewing arrangement to have Pasadena Lager in Los Angeles in time to be declared the "unofficial beer" of the Super Bowl on January 25, 1987. When the Pasadena brewery is built, it will brew a beer for the Rose Bowl held New Year's Day in the "City of the Roses."

Odjana is raising $2.5 million to build his brewery in a restored area of Pasadena. He hopes to have it built by the end of 1987.

Pasadena Lager

★   ★   ★

THE SAXTON BREWERY
11088 Midway
Chico, California 95926
    (916) 893-5637

President/Brewmaster: Dewayne L. Saxton
Founded: 1985
1986 Production: 100 barrels

The Saxton brewery prides itself on being the nation's smallest brewery, producing only 100 barrels of ale per year. The brewery is family run, with Dewayne brewmaster and wife Stacey in charge of administration.

Saxton's homebrewed ales won national awards including Best of Show (German-style Wheat Ale) at the 1984 American Homebrewers Convention; his English-style pilsner (Ivanhoe Ale) won its division at the 1985 AHA convention.

Saxton's ales are aged three months and have an alcohol content of 7%. Food-grade plastic containers are used for primary fermentation; secondary fermentation takes place in five-gallon glass carboys. The Saxtons bottle each batch by hand in 16 oz. recycleable German beer bottles.

Saxton says he gets his water for brewing from a cave 4,000 feet high in the Sierra Nevada Mountains 70 miles from Chico. He brews with malt extract and grain.

The Saxtons are planning on opening a brewpub, Colzaxx's Castle, in Chico in late 1987.

Ivanhoe Ale

Du Bru Ale

★   ★   ★

SIERRA NEVADA BREWING COMPANY
2539 Gilman Way
Chico, California 95926
   (916) 893-3520

Partners: Paul Camusi & Ken Grossman
Founded: 1978
1986 Production: 7,000 barrels

If there were medals given out for beer, Sierra Nevada would likely win for every category it entered. Paul Camusi and Ken Grossman started their small brewery in 1978 when most men their age (26 and 24 respectively) were just getting out of college and starting careers. Both had been serious homebrewers typical of the first generation of microbrewers in the late 1970s. They raised $110,000 from friends and family and began constructing their small brewery in 1979.

Camusi and Grossman chose Chico, a sleepy college town (California State College) in the foothills of the Sierra Nevada Mountains as the home for their brewery.

Camusi and Grossman were fortunate to have a mentor in Fritz Maytag of San Francisco's Anchor Brewing, who sold them equipment at more than fair prices. They also scrounged equipment from an old brewery, local dairies, and a creamery in Sacramento.

In 1983, Sierra Nevada Pale Ale and Porter won 1st and 2nd place at the Great American Beer Festival. Camusi and Grossman hope to reach 10,000 barrels by 1988 to satisfy the nationwide demand for their beer.

Sierra Nevada Pale Ale — *made from two-row pale and caramel malt, and Cascade, Clusters and Willamette hops.*

Sierra Nevada Porter — *made with a combination of pale, caramel, black patent malts, and Cascade, Clusters and Willamette hops.*

Sierra Nevada Big Foot Barley Wine — *brewed with pale and caramel malt, and Perles, Cascade, Northern Brewer, Clusters and Willamette hops.*

Sierra Nevada Celebration Ale — *has a rich, reddish hue and contains a mixture of hops including Nuggets, Chinook, Clusters, Cascade and Northern Brewer, which gives it a very distinctive aroma and taste.*

STANISLAUS BREWERY
3454 Shoemake Avenue
Modesto, California 95351
    (209) 523-2262

Partners: Garith and Romy Helms
Founded: 1984
1985 Production: 720 barrels

The Stanislaus Brewery is another California family brewery. The Helmses have relatives in the German brewing industry and in the mid-1970s, came upon the idea to brew Altbier, the old German beer that is still brewed in Dusseldorf but rarely exported to the U.S.

According to the Helmses, "Several hundred years ago, a monastic brewer named Brother Stan made 2 special "alt biers," an amber and a dark, to celebrate the 50-year reign of Frederick the Great. Brother Stan's "alt biers" were so unique that it was rumored the brews had been inspired by some divine being."

Stanislaus uses a German yeast to make their two "alt biers," which are neither pasteurized nor filtered. The beer is bottled in 1 liter bottles, "beer balls" and kegs for sale in East Bay and central California restaurants, bars and liquor stores. Seventy-five percent of St. Stans is sold on draft.

St. Stan's Amber — *a dry, full flavored amber beer with a creamy head.*

St. Stan's Dark — *a dark, heavy bodied beer with slight chocolaty taste similar to a porter.*

★   ★   ★

THOUSAND OAKS BREWERY
444 Vassar Avenue
Berkeley, California 94708
  (415) 525-8801

Partners: Charles and Diana Rixford
Founded: 1981
1986 Production: 228 barrels

Overlooking San Francisco's Golden Gate Bridge are the Berkeley Hills where middle-class homes line narrow streets near the Berkeley campus. In the basement of one of these homes is the Rixford family brewery that can't make up its mind to go commercial or remain a "cottage" brewery.

Father Charles, mother Diana, sons Steve, Allan, and daughter Christie brew tiny batches of their four beers from 52-gallon industrial barrels. Thousand Oaks beers are brewed in small quantities (up to 450 cases per month) which are sold in "gift packages," but not six-packs.

According to the Rixfords, theirs was the first commercial "home-brewery" in the U.S. when it opened in October 1981. They brew with malt extract.

All of the Thousand Oak labels are drawn by Christie, who is an artist. The Golden Gate label shows the famous bridge as it appears from the Rixfords' living room window.

Thousand Oaks Lager — *brewed with a partial mash of two-row Klages barley malt, Munich malt, dextrin and malt extract. The hops are Cascade pellets; the beer is fermented for four days, aged three weeks and is 5% alcohol by volume.*

Golden Gate Malt — *brewed with same basic ingredients as the Thousand Oaks lager, but with crystal malt and Yakima Clusters hops at a rate of 1.5 lb per gallon. The beer is 6% alcohol by volume.*

Golden Bear Malt Liquor — *is brewed with black patent malt, malt extract and Eroica hops. It is 6-6½% alcohol by volume.*

Cable Car Lager — *is made from Klages, dextrin, Munich malt and Galena hops.*

COLORADO

BOULDER BREWING COMPANY
2880 Wilderness Place
Boulder, Colorado 80301
(303) 444-8448

President: Jerry Smart
Founded: 1980
1986 Production: 4,700 barrels

After struggling from an ignoble beginning on a goat farm near Hygiene, Colorado, Boulder has moved into its new million-dollar cathedral-like brewery and launched aggressive marketing drives across the country.

In 1984, construction began on Boulder's new $1.4 million brewery, whose three-story high spires rise up as if to greet the famous Flatiron mountains, a local landmark, which serve as the logo on Boulder's labels. The new brewery is one of the most architecturally modern in America, complete with corporate offices, a small restaurant and outdoor patio.

With Boulder's increased capacity, a major drive was launched in 1985 to distribute in select markets around the country; Boulder is now sold in 23 states including California and Washington, D.C.

Boulder maintains a close relationship with the Coors brewery in nearby Golden, the largest brewery in America. Coors executives and brewers have provided time, expertise and spare equipment to help the state's "second-largest" brewery. Boulder even buys some of its malted barley from Coors.

Boulder Extra Pale Ale — *this light English-style ale is brewed with two-row pale and caramel malt, Cascade and Hallertauer hops.*

Boulder Porter — *brewed with pale, caramel and black malts; Cascade and Hallertauer hops. Alcohol content, 4.5% by volume.*

Boulder Christmas stout — *the brewery produces 1,100 cases of this rich, sweet stout for the holidays.*

Boulder Sport — *a new entry into the popular light beer market. The light lager has an attractive silver, green and blue label and is priced "to compete with Mexican and Canadian imports." Alcohol content, 3.45% by weight with 105 calories per bottle.*

TELLURIDE BEER COMPANY
Telluride, Colorado

President: Steve Patterson
Founded: 1986

Telluride produced its first beer in September 1986 with a small investment of $41,000 from 13 investors. Most of the beer is sold in the tiny town that becomes a popular ski resort in the winter.

Telluride contracts with the Huber brewery in Monroe, Wisconsin, to produce its beer. Distribution is done by Coors and Anheuser-Busch in Eastern Colorado.

Telluride Beer — *an amber lager brewed with dextrin, crystal, pale and black patent malt; Yakima, Hallertauer and Spalt hops.*

★　★　★

DISTRICT OF COLUMBIA

THE OLDE HEURICH BREWING CO.
1111 34th St. N. W.
Washington, D.C. 20007
(202) 333-2313

President: Gary Heurich
Brewmaster: Dr. Joseph Owades
Founded: 1986

Gary Heurich is the 28-year-old grandson of Christian Heurich, the founder of the largest and most historic brewery in the nation's capital. For the first half of the 20th century, the Heurich Brewery was a well-known landmark near the Lincoln Memorial and Heurich's German-style beers (including Old Georgetown and Senate beer) were local favorites. Christian Heurich was a generous philanthropist who lunched with Presidents, fielded sports teams and treated employees like family.

In 1945, at the age of 102, Heurich died and the brewery was taken over by son Christian, Jr., who ran it until 1956 when it closed. In 1962, the historic Heurich brewery was demolished to make way for the Kennedy Center and Watergate Hotel.

Gary Heurich was managing the family's real estate interests in the early 1980s when he began studying the growing microbrewing movement. He traveled to Germany, visited microbreweries and hired brewing consultant Dr. Joseph Owades who had already helped launch breweries in New York (New Amsterdam), Boston (Samuel Adams) and Philadelphia (Pennsylvania Pilsner).

In 1986, Heurich became the first microbrewer in America to reopen a family brewery when he introduced "Olde Heurich Amber Lager" to Washington. Heurich's attractive six-pack carton and advertising featuring Presidents Taft and Teddy Roosevelt holding new bottles of Heurich have won advertising awards.

Heurich is contract brewing at the Pittsburgh Brewery; he plans to build a brewery and museum in Washington by 1988.

Olde Heurich Amber Lager — *brewed with two-row American malting barley and a combination of Washington state (Cascade), Czechoslovakian (Saaz) and German (Hallertauer) hops.*

GEORGIA

SAVANNAH BEER COMPANY
126 Bay Street
Savannah, Georgia 31401
  (912) 232-0365

President: Alice Victor
Brewmaster: Dr. Joseph Owades
Founded: 1986

In 1984, Savannah urologist Dr. Irving Victor drank a bottle of New Amsterdam Amber Beer and was so impressed he hired Dr. Joseph Owades, who brewed New Amsterdam, and set up the Savannah Beer Company with his wife, Alice, as President.

The Victors contract brew XIII Colony (Georgia was the 13th colony) at Pittsburgh Brewing and distribute mainly in Atlanta and Savannah. Hilton Head, Charleston and Myrtle Beach will have XIII Colony by summer 1987.

XIII Colony Amber Beer — *brewed with two-row American malting barley, Hallertauer, Fuggles and Cascade hops.*

★　★　★

HAWAII

PACIFIC BREWING COMPANY
137 Mookua St.
Kailua, Hawaii 96734
  (808) 262-7664

President: Aloysius Klink
Brewmaster: Gunter Dittrich
Founded: 1986

Maui Lager is the first beer brewed in Hawaii since the Primo brewery closed in 1979.

Aloysius Klink's idea for a brewery came during a trip to visit his son who was working in a German brewery. Klink raised $2.5 million and hired fellow-German Gunter Dittrich as brewer.

The $2.5 million brewery is located in an old sugar mill.

Maui Lager — *brewed with Belgian malt, German hops and water from Maui's Iao Valley.*

IDAHO

SNAKE RIVER BREWING
Route 5, Box 30 A
Caldwell, Idaho 83605

President: Tim Batt
Founded: 1984
1986 Production: 151 barrels

Tim Batt, a veteran homebrewer, built his brewery in the middle of his family's hops and barley farm where all the Eroica and Galena hops in America are grown.

Natural disasters plagued Snake River in its early days. An earthquake weakened the brewery building in 1983, and in 1984 Batt had to use his first batch of beer to put out a fire in the brewery.

Amber Lager — *brewed with a variety of malts and Hallertauer hops.*

Premium Lager — *contains about 12% rice flakes making it similar in taste to standard American lagers.*

★   ★   ★

IOWA

MILLSTREAM BREWING COMPANY
P.O. Box 283
Amana, Iowa 52203
    (319) 622-3672

President: Carrol Zuber
Founded: 1985
1986 Production: 1,300 barrels

★   ★   ★

LOUISIANA

ABITA BREWING COMPANY
Route S, Box 174 A
Covington, Louisiana 70433
    (504) 893-3461

President: Rush Cumming
Founded: 1986

★   ★   ★

MAINE

D. L. GEARY BREWING COMPANY
38 Evergreen Drive
Portland, Maine 04103
   (207) 878-2337

President: David Geary
Brewer: Alan Pugsley
Founded: 1986

The Geary brewery sold the first beer brewed in a Maine brewery in December, 1986. David Geary raised $500,000 from a private stock issue to start his small brewery, which is located in an industrial park.

The brewery has a 24-barrel brewing capacity with production limited to draft keg beer for taverns and restaurants; a bottling line is planned for 1987.

Geary's Pale Ale

★   ★   ★

MAINE COAST BREWING
P.O. Box 1118
Portland, Maine 04104
   (207) 773-7970

Founders: Jon Bove/Hugh Nazor
Founded: 1986

Until Jon Bove and partner Hugh Nazor raise $1.5 million to build their brewery in Maine, they are contract-brewing with Hibernia in Eau Claire, Wisconsin.

Wives Lynn and Linda left their jobs to work with their husbands on the brewery. Six-packs of Portland Lager contain the names of the husbands at one end, the wives at the other.

Portland Lager

★   ★   ★

MASSACHUSETTS

THE BOSTON BEER COMPANY
30 Germania St.
Boston, Massachusetts 02130
   (617) 522-3400

President: Jim Koch
Brewmaster: Dr. Joseph Owades
Founded: 1985

Jim Koch is riding a whirlwind he created in 1985 when he started selling his Samuel Adams Boston Lager. Two months after he introduced his beer, it won "Most Popular Beer" at the Great American Beer Festival.

Koch is typical of the second generation of microbrewers who came to their calling from a professional career in an unrelated field. Koch graduated from Harvard with an MBA and law degree and went to work for The Boston Consulting Group that reportedly paid him $200,00 per year as a management consultant.

But Koch had brewing in his blood; every eldest Koch son, going back five generations, had been brewers. Koch became the sixth when he hired Dr. Joseph Owades as his consultant.

Koch followed the strategy of Matthew Reich in New York by targeting the best restaurants, hotels and saloons in Boston to carry Samuel Adams. Winning "Most Popular Beer" in 1985 attracted attention and Koch lost no time getting his name — and Samuel Adams — before the national media. *People Magazine* and *Business Week* wrote about Koch's bold introduction into the rank of American microbrewers and he appeared on the McNeil-Lehrer News Hour.

Koch is as much a revolutionary as the namesake of his beer. In 1986, Samuel Adams became the first American beer to pass the German Reinheitsbegot purity law and be exported into Germany.

Koch introduced his beer to Washington, D.C. in 1986 and staged another coup when the White House asked to have Samuel Adams delivered to the White House Mess, Air Force One and Camp David.

The Boston Beer Company's offices are in the old Haffenreffer Brewery, where Koch hopes to open his brewery in 1987 or 1988.

Samuel Adams Boston Lager — *two-row American malting barley, Tettnang and Hallertauer hops.*

MINNESOTA

SUMMIT BREWING COMPANY
St. Paul, Minnesota

President: Mark Stutrud
Founded: 1986

Mark Stutrud raised $600,000 to buy brewing equipment from Germany and Minnesota to start his brewery, which opened in September 1986 and sells only keg draft beer. A bottling line is planned for 1987.

Summit Pale Ale — *brewed with pale and caramel malt; and Eroica, Cascade and Fuggles hops.*

★   ★   ★

FITGER'S BREWING COMPANY
Duluth, Minnesota

Partner: Paul Nelson
Founded: 1984

The original Fitger's Brewery closed in 1972 but was reopened as part of a hotel complex on Lake Superior. Fitger's is sold in Northern Minnesota and "exported" south to the Twin Cities and Wisconsin. Fitger's is contract brewed at Huber Brewing in Monroe, Wisconsin.

Fitger's Super Premium Export — *brewed with four malts, Spalt, Hallertauer and Yakima hops.*

★   ★   ★

MICHIGAN

KALAMAZOO BREWING COMPANY
P.O. Box 1674
315 E. Kalamazoo Avenue
Kalamazoo, Michigan 49007
    (616) 382-2338

President/Brewmaster: Larry J. Bell
Founded: 1985
1986 Production: 135 barrels

Kalamazoo's Great Lakes Amber Ale is only available locally.

MONTANA

MONTANA BEVERAGE, LTD. (KESSLER BREWING)
1439 Harris Street
Helena, Montana 59601
    (406) 449-6214

President: Bruce DeRosier
Brewmaster: Julius Hummer
Founded: 1984
1986 Production: 2,000 barrels

Kessler was once the most historic brewery in Montana founded in 1865 by two gold miners, Nicholas Kessler and Charles Beehrer, in Last Chance Gulch (later renamed Helena, now the state capital). Kessler and Beehrer were also bakers and brewers (and part-time vigilantes) who followed Montana gold miners in the 1860s.

Bruce DeRosier, a Helena wine distributor and his partner, Dick Bourke, obtained the rights to the Kessler name and reopened the brewery after a 20-year drought of brewing in Montana. They hired Dan Carey, a young San Francisco brewmaster recently graduated from the University of California School of Brewing at Davis, who preferred making specialty beers to working for larger breweries.

DeRosier and Bourke raised approximately $250,000 from investors and purchased old dairy equipment from Montana farmers to get started. Lacking a large population in its homestate, Kessler seeks to develop a following in resorts of Sun Valley, Jackson Hole, and the college towns of Missoula and Bozeman, Montana, and Spokane, Washington.

Responding to consumers' request for a lighter summer beer, Kessler brewed Lorelei in 1986, one of the original Kessler beers.

Kessler Lager — *a European style lager.*

Lorelei Extra Pale — *a pale, golden lager.*

Kessler Bock — *dark lager with slight toffee flavor.*

Kessler Wheat — *rich, mahogany color with fruity flavor.*

Kessler Oktoberfest — *Munich style copper-colored lager.*

Kessler Holiday — *sweet, amber beer with slight spicy taste.*

NEW JERSEY

VERNON VALLEY BREWERY
P.O. Box 1100 Rt. 94
Vernon, New Jersey 07462
  (201) 827-0034

President: Owen Davis
Brewmaster: Stefan Muhs
Founded: 1985

Vernon Valley is a ski resort and theme park near New York City. Partners Davis and Angelo Gibalaisco borrowed $500,000 to buy brewing equipment from Germany and signed a long-term lease with the resort.

Three German-style beers are brewed.

★　★　★

NEW YORK

WILLIAM S. NEWMAN BREWING COMPANY
32 Learned Street
Albany, New York 12207
   (518) 465-8501

Partners: William and Marie Newman
Founded: 1982
1985 Production: 4,608 barrels

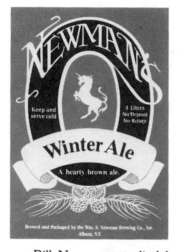

Bill and Marie Newman run the longest operating man-and-wife microbrewery in the U.S. When they opened the Newman Brewing Company, the Newmans were considered too eccentric and idealistic to succeed. Not only were they starting a small brewery, but they were doing it in the state capital.

The Newmans have achieved special status as veteran and highly-respected microbrewers. Their survival is a testament to their energy, determination and brewing skill. In 1984 and 1985, their ales finished in the top 10 at the Great American Beer Festival.

Bill Newman studied brewing at the Ringwood Brewery and took courses at the Brewers Academy in Connecticut. The Newmans secured a small-business loan from Albany, another loan from a local bank and used savings to raise $250,000 to open their brewery in 1982.

To start out, the Newmans brewed only keg beer. They later added half kegs, quarter kegs, four-liter plastic containers and even gallon take-home mugs. They didn't bottle their beer until 1985 when they arranged to contract-brew a lager beer at Hibernia in Eau Claire, Wisconson. In 1986, they switched to the Schmidt Brewing Company outside Philadelphia for their contract-brewed lager.

Newman's Albany Amber Ale — *pale, caramel and black patent malts, Yakima Clusters and Fuggles hops. An English-style ale, quite hoppy and full bodied.*

Newman's Albany Amber Beer — *this is the contract-brewed lager made with pale and roasted malt, Yakima Clusters and Fuggles hops.*

OLD NEW YORK BREWING COMPANY
(NEW AMSTERDAM BREWERY AND TAPROOM)
610 West 26th St.
New York, New York 10001
  (212) 255-4100

President: Matthew Reich
Brewmaster: Dr. Joseph Owades
Founded: 1982
1985 Production: 9,000 barrels

Matthew Reich is one of the pioneers in American microbrewing. When Reich left his job as lending officer with Citibank in 1982 to start a microbrewery, he was heading into uncharted waters on the East Coast. The Newman Brewery in Albany was starting up, but selling a new beer in Manhattan was a much more ambitious task.

After Reich hired Dr. Joseph Owades to help him design a beer, he found 22 investors and raised $250,000 to begin brewing at the West End Brewery in upstate Utica. Once Reich's beer was available, he visited hundreds of Manhattan restaurants, liquor stores, hotels and taverns to get them to carry his new beer. Many long-time bartenders compared Reich's New Amsterdam Amber Beer to Rheingold and Trommers, two popular beers in New York before Manhattan lost its last brewery in 1976.

Through Reich's hard work, New Amsterdam became popular in Manhattan's trendiest restaurants and sold for $3.50 per bottle in some establishments. After the market had been established for New Amsterdam, Reich raised $2.5 million to build his New Amsterdam Brewery and Taproom, which opened in October 1985 with Mayor Ed Koch and numerous Manhattan celebrities attending the ceremonies.

New Amsterdam is now carried at more than 1,400 outlets in New York and in 22 states, the District of Columbia and Canada. In 1986, Reich's beer was exported to Great Britain.

Reich's example of marketing has been duplicated in Boston (Samuel Adams), Philadelphia (Pennsylvania Pilsner) and Washington, D.C. (Olde Heurich). Dr. Joseph Owades was consultant for the ventures, which are all contract-brewed.

New Amsterdam Amber Beer — *brewed with two-row American malting barley, Hallertauer and Cascade hops.*

OREGON

WIDMER BREWING COMPANY
1405 N.W. Lovejoy
Portland, Oregon 97209
   (503) 227-7276

Brewmaster: Kurt Widmer
Founded: 1985

The Widmer family — father Ray and brothers Kurt and Robert — is the Widmer Brewery. The three Widmers put together an assorted collection of equipment from a variety of sources including an old dairy and an abandoned nuclear plant to start their brewery. Their resourcefulness enabled them to open their brewery at about half the $250-400,000 normally required for most microbreweries.

The Widmer microbrewery is one of two American micros (Stanislaus in Modesto, California is the other) that brews German alt beer.

The Widmer brewery is located in a city that boasts more breweries (seven) than any other city in the United States. Four of the Portland breweries (Blitz-Weinhard, Portland, Columbia and Widmer) are located within a half-mile of each other in the industrial northwest section of the city (the other three are brewpubs owned by Mike McMenamin).

Widmer Alt — *pale, Munich, caramel and black malts; Oregon Perle and Tettnanger hops. This is the flagship beer of Widmer.*

Widmer Weizen — *the same malts, but with wheat added; Tettnanger and Cascade hops.*

Widmer Oktoberfest — *an amber-colored beer brewed with Haller-tauer hops; brewed from September to November.*

Widmer Fest — *pale, caramel and Munich malts; Perle and Tettnanger hops. Brewed in December and January.*

Widmer Maerzen — *pale, Munich and dextrin malt; Tettnanger and Hallertauer hops.*

Widmer Bock — *pale, Munich, dextrin and caramel malt; Hallertauer, Perle and Tettnanger hops. Brewed from June through August.*

PENNSYLVANIA

DOCK STREET BREWING COMPANY
P.O. Box 30255
Philadelphia, Pennsylvania 19103
    (215) 789-3625

President: Jeffrey D. Ware
Brewmaster: Mort Brenner
Founded: 1986

Philadelphia's Dock Street was once home to colonial taverns with such colorful names as The Blue Anchor, Turk's Head, Indian Queen, Penny Pot and Golden Lion. At the nearby City Tavern, George Washington met Lafayette and Thomas Jefferson drank ale during the Continental Congress.

Jeffrey Ware, a one-time chef, is capitalizing on Philadelphia's love of tradition by naming his brewery after the historic area.

Before Ware started his brewery, he studied the brewing history of Philadelphia, which once was home to 100 breweries. In September 1986, Ware introduced Dock Street to Philadelphia; the next month, his beer was voted one of the Top Ten beers at the Great American Beer Festival.

Ware's brewing consultant was Mort Brenner, who worked for 40 years in breweries all over the world. Ware contract brews at the West End Brewery in Utica, New York. Initial production will be 2,500 barrels per year with distribution largely in Pennsylvania's Delaware Valley.

Dock Street Amber Beer — *an ale brewed with 2-row malt and Cascade hops.*

PENNSYLVANIA BREWING COMPANY
The Bourse - Suite 900 W
Independence Mall
Philadelphia, Pennsylvania 19106
    (215) 625-9501

President: Thomas V. Pastorius
Brewmaster: Dr. Joseph Owades
Founded: 1986

Pennsylvania has a long and historic tradition of brewing, and Tom Pastorius is missing few opportunities to provide an authentic German-style beer to the large population of Germans in Pennsylvania.

Pastorius' family was one of the first German families to arrive in America, and his descendants founded Germantown, Pennsylvania, in 1683. Pastorius spent 12 years in Germany as a consultant and still makes monthly business trips to Frankfurt.

The model for Pastorius' beer came from the Erbacker brewery near Heidelberg. Pennsylvania Pilsner even passed the German Reinheitsgebot purity law, which means it contains no antioxidants, foam stabilizers, preservatives or other additives.

Pastorius contract-brews at Pittsburgh Brewing with Dr. Joseph Owades as his consultant. Pennsylvania Pilsner is sold in eastern Pennsylvania and New Jersey.

Pastorius is in the process of converting the old Eberhardt & Ober Brewery in Pittsburgh into an authentic German "Brauerei Gasthof" brewpub.

Pennsylvania Pilsner — *brewed with 2-row malt, Hallertauer and Tettnang hops.*

★   ★   ★

TEXAS

REINHEITSGEBOT BREWING COMPANY
1107 Summit #2
Plano, Texas 75074
   (214) 423-5484

Owners: Don and Mary Thompson
Brewmaster: Don Thompson
Founded: 1985
1985 Production: 260 barrels

Texas' first microbrewery is located in a warehouse in the Dallas suburb of Plano, run by a young couple, Don and Mary Thompson, who met while camping in Morocco in the late 1970s.

After returning to the U.S. and marrying, Don and Mary tried a variety of jobs while Don became involved in homebrewing. After he won Homebrewer of the Year in 1982, they agreed it was time to get serious about going commercial with Don's brewing. They purchased old brewing equipment from the Spoetzl Brewery, which makes Shiner beer in Texas.

The Thompsons named their brewery after the 1516 German purity law and their beer after their home county. Texas law even lets them distribute in Don's battered Volkswagen bus. Their main markets are Plano, Dallas and neighboring suburbs.

Collin County Pure Gold — *light lager, dry hopped with Hallertauer hops, producing 4% alcohol.*

Collin County Black Gold — *half of this lager is roasted Munich malt plus caramel malt; not as hoppy as Pure Gold.*

★　　★　　★

VERMONT

CATAMOUNT BREWING COMPANY
58 S. Main
White River Junction, Vermont 05001
   (802) 296-2248

President/Brewmaster: Stephen Mason
Founded: 1986

The Catamount Brewery, Vermont's first microbrewery, is located on the border with New Hampshire and has an eye on Boston — America's second-largest import beer market — as a prime market for its beer.

Steve Mason and Alan Davis, both former Vermont teachers, started their small brewery with $230,000 obtained through a private stock offering, a $115,000 Small Business Administration loan, and a $85,000 low-interest loan from the state. Mason left his teaching job in 1983 and went off to learn brewing at the Swannell brewery in England and the Newman brewery in Albany, New York.

The brewery is housed in an old Swift meat-packing plant and has a 28-barrel brewing capacity. Catamount will produce about 2,000 barrels in its first full year of production in 1987.

Time magazine featured the Catamount Brewery in a February 1987 essay on "Making Beer the Old-Fashioned Way." The essay said Catamount Amber "is red in cast, bread fresh, with the body of a weight lifter: serious beer."

Catamount Amber — *this copper-colored, British-style ale is brewed with American six-row and crystal malting barley, Galena and Willamette hops.*

Catamount Gold — *brewed with 100% malting barley and Willamette hops.*

VIRGINIA

CHESAPEAKE BAY BREWING COMPANY
1373 London Bridge Road
Virgina Beach, Virginia 23456
   (604) 472-5230

President: Michael Hollingsworth
Brewmaster: Wolfgang Roth
1986 Production: 1,720 barrels

In August 1986, Michael Hollingsworth purchased 93% of the stock of Chesapeake Brewing from founders Jim and Frank Kollar.

In the early 1980s, Jim Kollar was a Tidewater veterinarian and ambitious homebrewer who spent five years building his small brewery. His method was much different than most American microbrewers. Kollar bought land, new brewing equipment, built his brewery in an industrial park and traveled to Germany to hire 26-year-old brewer Wolfgang Roth. These early ventures took up much of Kollar's pre-brewing capital, and for the two years his brewery was operating he was always searching out investors.

One marketing decision that also hindered Kollar was his far-flung distribution network which extended from Pennsylvania to North Carolina. Most American microbreweries have concentrated on a small area in the beginning and then expand distribution when their beer has established a following.

Chesbay brews a house brand for the newly re-opened Occidental Restaurant in Washington, D.C., one block from the White House. In its earlier life, the Occidental was the most famous restaurant in Washington whose patrons included Thomas Edison, Charles Lindbergh, John D. Rockefeller, Buffalo Bill, Winston Churchill and every President since 1906.

Chesbay was voted one of the top ten beers at the Great American Beer Festival in 1985 and 1986.

Chesbay Amber — *a combination of American barley malt, crystal malt and hop pellets. This is a slightly dark, Munich-style lager with 4% alcohol.*

Chesbay Gold — *a lighter Pilsner style, also 4% alcohol.*

Schooner Doppelbock — *Chesbay's first special brew takes 3½ months to brew; contains 6% alcohol.*

WASHINGTON

HALE'S ALES, LTD.
410 N. Washington
Colville, Washington 99114
   (509) 684-6503

President/Brewmaster: Mike Hale
Founded: 1983
1985 Production: 1,400 barrels

Hale's Ales is as close to a one-man operation as there is in microbrewing. That one man is Mike Hale, a transplanted Californian who fell in love with the serenity and rugged individualism in Northeast Washington. Hale is a former electrician and horticulturist who served on the Colville city council and is now the town's brewer.

In the early 1980s, Hale traveled to England and fell in love with English ales. He lived there for most of 1981, working in breweries and learning the craft of small-scale ale brewing. When he returned to Colville, Hale acquired a warehouse and did the wiring, plumbing, and construction to install his small brewery. According to Hale, his brewery cost less than $100,000 by the time it opened in 1983, producing the first kegs of Hale's American Ale.

A second Hale's brewery is projected to open across Washington state in the Seattle suburb of Kirkland, one of Hale's prime markets. Hale's markets are upscale restaurants in Spokane, Portland, Seattle and the Idaho panhandle. Hale has only three part-time employees; he does everything from brewing to cleaning up, and even driving the van that carries his beer across the state.

Hale's Pale American Ale — *an English-style bitter made from Canadian Klages two-row malt, Cascade and Clusters hops. Fermenting takes place at 62 degrees for four days and the ale is cold stored for nine days before kegging.*

Hale's Special Bitter — *similar to the Pale American Ale, but contains more crystal malt and hops.*

Hale's Celebration Ale — *first brewed in January 1985 when the brewery celebrated its 1,000th barrel of beer. The darkest, heaviest and smoothest of Hale's beers.*

HART BREWING
176 First Avenue
Kalama, Washington 98625
(206) 673-2962

Partners: Tom Baune and Beth Hartwell
Brewer: Tom Baune
Founded: 1984
1985 Production: 550 barrels

Tom Baune worked for Weyerhaeuser in western Washington until he was laid off in the late 1970s recession. Baune and his wife, Beth Hartwell, operated a small delicatessen in Seattle before moving back to Kalama near the Columbia River to open their family brewery.

The Hart Brewery, named after wife Beth, is located in a main street general store that Tom and Beth bought in 1986. The building still resembles a general store with empty kegs, six-pack cartons, labels and assorted boxes filling the front of the building. In the rear are the brewkettle, fermentation tanks, cold storage tank and new Italian bottling line.

Water for Hart's ales comes from glacier runoff from Mount St. Helens 35 miles northeast of Kalama. The first beer brewed by Hart in September 1984, was Pyramid Ale; Hart followed with Pyramid Wheaten Ale in May 1985, the first draft wheat beer in the U.S.

Hart's Pyramid Ale was rated "Best Beer of 1984" and "Best of Show" in 1986 by Portland beer writer Fred Eckhardt. Eckhardt considers the beer "one of the finest beers in the world."

Pyramid Pale Ale — *two-row and caramel malts; Cascade cone hops. This is one of the hoppiest ales brewed.*

Pyramid Wheaten Ale — *brewed with 50% wheat and pale two-row malt; Cascade, Hallertauer and Herschbrucker hops.*

Pyramid Special Dark Ale — *pale, wheat, roasted wheat, caramel malt, roasted malt; Cascade and Hallertauer cone hops.*

St. Nick's Special Ale — *pale two-row and wheat malt, caramel malt, roasted malt; Cascade and Hallertauer cone hops. The seasonal Hart Ale, it has cardamom added for a spicy taste.*

Pacific Crest — *a lighter hopped version of Pale Ale.*

INDEPENDENT ALE BREWERY (RED HOOK BREWING)
4620 Leary Way Northwest
Seattle, Washington 98107
(206) 784-0800

President: Paul Shipman
Brewmaster: Rick Buchanan
Founded: 1982
1986 Production: 5,990 barrels

Paul Shipman was a marketing representative for the Chateau Ste. Michelle winery in 1977 when he met Seattle entrepreneur Gordon Bowker. Their friendship led to discussions about opening a brewery. They raised $350,000 and in August 1982, they opened the Independent Ale Brewery, Seattle's first brewery in 35 years.

The brewery is located in the Ballard industrial area of Seattle's ship canal near a Scandinavian neighborhood. Shipman even named one of his beers, Ballard Bitter, in honor of the Scandinavians. The slogan on the label, "Ya sure ya betcha!", is adopted from a local high school football cheer ("Lutefisk, lefsa; We're gonna beat ya! Ya sure ya betcha!") The slogan refers to two Norwegian foods, lutefisk (a dried codfish) and lefsa (a soft bread made from potatoes) and an expression popular among Norwegians. Ballard Bitter was introduced on May 17, Norwegian Constitution Day.

The brewery includes a Hospitality Room where customers can sample three ales on tap or buy T-shirts, hats and six-packs of fresh beer.

Redhook Ale — *two-row, pale, caramel and black patent malt; Yakima Eroica, Oregon Willamette, and English East Kent Goldings hops. Redhook has a reddish color and is slightly sweet and spicy. Michael Jackson, the English beer expert, pronounced Redhook a "Belgian-style ale," when he first tasted it and the brewery has used the term ever since to indicate its uniqueness.*

Blackhook Porter — *pale, caramel, black patent and roasted malts; Clusters, Cascade and Eroica hops. It has a pleasant coffee-like flavor.*

Ballard Bitter — *pale and caramel malt; Clusters, Eroica and Cascade hops. Similar to an English style bitter.*

Winterhook Christmas ale — *pale and caramel malts; Fuggles and Tettnang hops. First introduced in December 1985.*

THOMAS KEMPER BREWING
P.O. Box 4689
Rollingbay, Washington 98061
   (206) 842-7837

Partners: Will and Mari Kemper/Andy Thomas
Brewmaster: Will Kemper
Founded: 1985
1986 Production: 1,000 barrels

Will Kemper was a chemical engineer in the early 1980s who became disenchanted as a consultant for a hazardous waste clean-up firm with contracts from the Environmental Protection Agency. Rather than be a bureaucrat, Kemper opted to turn his homebrewing experience — as well as his background in chemistry — into a career as a microbrewer.

Along with wife Mari and friend Andy Thomas, the three of them started the Thomas Kemper microbrewery in January 1985 on Bainbridge Island across the sound from Seattle. The brewery, located in an industrial park, consists mostly of used dairy equipment; it produces only draft keg beer, but a bottling line is planned with the first expansion in 1987.

Thomas Kemper produces a *heles* lager, an amber-colored Munich-style lager which is darker and sweeter than conventional lagers. Water for brewing comes from melted snow of Washington's Olympic Range.

Kemper has about 100 outlets in western Washington, most in the Seattle area. Future plans include larger facilities to accommodate a "biergarten," delicatessen, retail outlet, and bottling line.

Thomas Kemper Munchener Helles — *pale, Munich, caramel and black patent malts; Yakima Clusters, Cascade and Hallertauer hops. The special yeast gives this lager the fruity taste of an ale.*

Thomas Kemper Dunkel — *the same malts and hops with more black patent malt to create a darker color and roasted taste.*

★   ★   ★

KUEFNERBRAU
112 N. Lewis Street
Monroe, Washington 98272
    (206) 784-4186

Founder/Brewmaster: Robert Kuefner
Founded: 1984

The Kuefnerbrau is a one-person operation. Robert Kuefner is a former Bavarian brewmaster who moved to the U.S. and became a brewer for Anheuser-Busch. He later moved to Washington and started his own brewery, the smallest in the Northwest.

Kuefner began brewing with malt extract but changed to all-grain brewing in 1985. His Old Bavarian Style Beer is sold in Seattle and western Washington.

Old Bavarian Style — *brewed with two-row pale malt, caramel malt and hops from British Columbia and the Yakima Valley.*

★   ★   ★

SMITH & REILLY
Vancouver, Washington

President: Jim Smith
Founded: 1986

This is a contract brewing arrangment with the Pabst Olympia brewery in Tumwater, Washington. The beer, an all-malt lager, is targeted at import lager drinkers. Most Northwest microbreweries and brewpubs produce ales.

Smith and Reilly Honest beer is bottled.

★   ★   ★

WISCONSIN

CAPITAL BREWING COMPANY
434 State St.
Madison, Wisconsin 53703
    (608) 257-0099

President: Ed Janus
Founded: 1986

HIBERNIA BREWING COMPANY
318 Elm Street
Eau Claire, Wisconsin 54703
  (715) 836-2337
President: Michael Healy
Brewer: John Walter
Founded: 1985

Michael Healy was vice president of a bank note company in Chicago in the early 1980s when he fell in love with the idea of owning his own brewery. He visited breweries all over the country while on business trips and along the way heard that a small brewery in Eau Claire, Wisconsin, was about to go under.

Healy visited the Walter Brewery, where brewing was done only one day a week and closure was imminent. Healy mortgaged two houses, sold his favorite antique car, a 1936 Auburn roadster, and cashed in his stock and retirement funds. With a federal small business loan, Healy purchased the brewery and renamed it Hibernia (old Ireland) in honor of his heritage. Healy also hired Alan Dikty, editor of *New Brewer* magazine, as marketing director and the two of them set out to turn the old Walter brewery into one that brewed specialty beers. The first year of operation, Hibernia's Dunkel Weizen Beer was voted the top specialty beer at the 1985 Great American Beer Festival.

Healy also restored a vacant lot near the brewery that had once been a biergarten and renamed it "Walter Park." (See American brewpub directory.)

Eau Claire All Malt Lager

Hibernia Bock

Dunkel Weizen

Oktober Fest

Winter Brau

★   ★   ★

SPRECHER BREWING COMPANY
730 W. Oregon St.
Milwaukee, Wisconsin 53204
(414) 272-2337

President/Brewmaster: Randy Sprecher
Founded: 1986
1986 Production: 988 barrels

Randy Sprecher developed a love for good beer on a military tour in Germany and later went to work for Pabst in Milwaukee. When the brewery was sold in 1984, Sprecher used his life savings, loans and money from investors to start his brewery in an old tannery on Milwaukee's South Side.

Sprecher's production is limited to kegs and 1 liter ceramic bottles. The brewery's annual 1,000 barrel production is sold to taverns and restaurants around Milwaukee; an expansion is underway to increase production.

Sprecher Amber

Black Bavarian

Milwaukee Weiss beer

★   ★   ★

VIENNA BREWING COMPANY
5325 W. Burleigh Street
Milwaukee, Wisconsin 53212
(414) 449-9705

President: Gary Bauer
Founded: 1986

Gary Bauer was a homebrew supply shop owner and award-winning homebrewer whose beer won Best of Show for European lagers at the 1985 Great American Beer Festival.

In 1986, Bauer established his brewery and began contract brewing his specialty beer, Vienna-style lager, at the Eau Claire Hibernia Brewery. Vienna Lager is reddish in color and made with roasted malts. Bauer says he translated German brewing records to come up with the authentic recipe for his beer.

Vienna is now contract-brewed at the Huber Brewery in Monroe, Wisconsin. Vienna Lager won the Chicago Beer Society's 10th annual International Beer Tasting in 1986.

Vienna Lager — *brewed with Vienna malt, three other malts, Hallertauer and Spalt hops. The beer is aged a full eight weeks at 32 degrees F. The alcohol content is 5% by volume.*

★   ★   ★

PREVIEWS OF COMING ATTRACTIONS

ALASKA

CHINOOK ALASKAN BREWING AND BOTTLING COMPANY
Douglas, Alaska

Brewmaster: Geoff Larson

JV Northwest is the supplier for Alaska's first microbrewery, scheduled to open in 1987.

★   ★   ★

CALIFORNIA

CROWN CITY BREWERY
181 East Alegria Avenue
Sierra Madre, California 91024
(818) 355-7914

Founder: Mike Lanzarotta

★   ★   ★

GOLDEN PACIFIC BREWING COMPANY
Emeryville, California

Partners: Maureen Logo and Tad Stratford
Founded: 1986

★   ★   ★

NORTH COAST BREWING COMPANY
1162 Buttermilk Lane
Arcata, California 95521

Founder: Steve McHaney

★   ★   ★

XCELSIOR BREWERY
511 Wilson Street
Santa Rosa, California 95401
    (707) 578-1497

President: Pete Eierman
Brewmaster: Brian Hunt

The Xcelsior brewery is in a renovated railroad station in a part of downtown Santa Rosa experiencing economic revival. The area has many attractions popular with tourists and visitors — theaters, restaurants, shops, art galleries and the Sonoma County Museum. Santa Rosa is one of the stops for visitors to northern California wineries.

The brewery purchased the rights to the Acme name, once one of California's most popular beers before Prohibition. The old Acme label has been redesigned in a colorful art deco fashion.

Vice-president John Senkevich will draw on his experience as a Northern California wine distributor to distribute Acme beer when it becomes available in 1987.

★   ★   ★

MINNESOTA

JAMES PAGE BREWING COMPANY
1300 Quincy Street N.E.
Minneapolis, Minnesota 55413
    (612) 331-2833

Founder: James Page

The first beer from this brewery, Old St. Anthony's Lager, is supposed to roll out the door in 1987. The beer will be available in kegs for Minneapolis tavern and restaurants.

St. Anthony Village was the site of a German brewery in Minneapolis in the 1850s. Specialty beers, including James Page Private Stock, are planned.

★   ★   ★

PENNSYLVANIA

EBERHARD & OBER BREWING COMPANY
Vinial Street and Mount Troy Road
Pittsburgh, Pennsylvania

Founder: Thomas Pastorius

In 1986, Tom Pastorius purchased Pittsburgh's old Eberhard & Ober Brewery which had closed in 1952. The old brewery cost $170,000 and will be renovated in a $3.5 million project to include a high-tech office complex. The project is jointly funded by Pittsburgh's North Side Civic Development Council and has received zoning approval for the brewery and office complex.

Pastorius already has a contract brewing arrangement with Pittsburgh Brewing to brew his Pennsylvania Pilsner for the Philadelphia and eastern Pennsylvania markets. He will brew ales and stouts at his Pittsburgh Eberhard & Ober Brewery, but can't sell Pennsylvania Pilsner at the new brewery because of his arrangement with Pittsburgh Brewing.

★　★　★

1985
GREAT AMERICAN BEER FESTIVAL
MOST POPULAR BEERS IN AMERICA
May 31 - June 1, 1985
Denver, Colorado

1. Samuel Adams Boston Lager
   (Boston Beer Company; founded 1985)

2. Hibernia Dunkel Weizen Fest Beer
   (Hibernia Brewing, Eau Claire, Wisconsin; 1985)

3. Snake River Amber Lager
   (Snake River Brewing, Caldwell, Idaho; 1984)

4. New Amsterdam Amber Beer
   (Old New York Brewing, New York; 1982)

5. White Tail Lager
   (Arkansas Brewery, Little Rock, Arkansas; 1984. Went out of business in 1986)

6. Grant's Imperial Stout
   (Yakima Brewing & Malting, Yakima, Washington; 1982)

7. Newman's Albany Amber Ale
   (Newman Brewing, Albany, New York; 1982)

8. (tie) Chesbay Amber
   (Chesapeake Bay Brewing, Virginia Beach, Virginia; 1984)

   Thomas Kemper Lager
   (Kemper Brewing, Bainbridge Island, Washington; 1985)

10. Redhook Ale
    (Independent Brewing, Seattle, Washington; 1982)

Designation of Most Popular Beer is by balloting of ticket holders to the two nights of the Great American Beer Festival. Many brewers object to the popular balloting since there is no official judging or formal tasting rules. As a result, there have been complaints in recent years about the "electioneering" that goes on, including handing out free hats and T-shirts and the numbers of young women hired to promote and serve beer at the breweries' booths.

The American Homebrewers Association, which sponsors the GABF every year in Denver, has stated that measures will be taken in 1987 to stem the aggressive campaigning which gives the festival the appearance of a political convention.

1986
GREAT AMERICAN BEER FESTIVAL
MOST POPULAR BEERS IN AMERICA
October 2-3, 1986
Denver, Colorado

1. Samuel Adams Boston Lager* ***
   (Boston Beer, Boston, Massachusetts; founded 1985)

2. Fest Beer
   (Boulder Brewing, Boulder, Colorado; 1980)

3. Dock Street Amber Beer* **
   (Dock Street Brewing; Philadelphia, Pennsylvania; 1986)

4. Pennsylvania Pilsner* **
   (Pennsylvania Brewing, Philadelphia, Pennsylvania; 1986)

5. Portland Lager* **
   (Maine Coast Brewing, Portland, Maine; 1986)

6. XIII Colony* **
   (Savannah Brewing, Savannah, Georgia; 1986)

7. Schooner Double Bock
   (Chesapeake Bay Brewing, Virginia Beach, Virginia; 1984)

8. Vienna Style Lager* **
   (Vienna Brewing, Milwaukee, Wisconsin; 1986)

9. Olde Heurich Amber Lager* **
   (Olde Heurich Brewing, Washington, D.C.; 1986)

10. India Pale Ale
    (Yakima Brewing, Yakima, Washington; 1982)

   * Contract breweries (four with Dr. Joseph Owades as brewing consultant).

  ** Six of the breweries started up in 1986: Dock Street, Pennsylvania Pilsner, Portland, XIII Colony, Vienna, Olde Heurich.

 *** Repeated as Most Popular Beer 1985 & 1986.

1987
GREAT AMERICAN BEER FESTIVAL
MOST POPULAR BEERS IN AMERICA
June 5 - June 6, 1987
Denver, Colorado

1. Samuel Adams Festival Lager* **
   (Boston Beer, Boston, Massachusetts; founded 1985)

2. 1987 Boulder Festival Brew***
   (Boulder Brewing, Boulder, Colorado; 1980)

3. Chinook Alaskan Amber Beer
   (Chinook Alaskan Brewing, Douglas, Alaska; 1987)

4. Thomas Kemper Helles
   (Kemper Brewing, Rolling Bay, Washington; 1985)

5. Pete's Wicked Ale*
   (Pete's Brewing, Palo Alto, California; 1987)

6. Dock Street Amber Beer*
   (Dock Street Brewing, Havertown, Pennsylvania; 1986)

7. Telluride Beer*
   (Telluride Beer, Telluride, Colorado; 1986)

8. Grant's Imperial Stout
   (Yakima Brewing and Malting, Yakima, Washington; 1982)

9. Sierra Nevada Bigfoot Barley Wine Style Ale
   (Sierra Nevada Brewing, Chico, California; 1978)

10. Olde Heurich Amber Lager*
    (Olde Heurich Brewing, Washington, D.C.; 1986)

  * Contract breweries.

 ** Boston Beer repeated as winner for third straight year in the consumer preference poll with a new beer, Festival Lager. Boston's Samuel Adams, the winner in 1985 and 1986 poll was judged the winner in the continental pilsener category by the professional tasting panel.

*** Boulder Festival Brew finished second for the second straight year in the consumer preference poll. Boulder Stout won the Stout category in the professional tasting panel; Boulder Porter placed second in the porter category.

A DIRECTORY OF AMERICAN BREWPUBS

One of the most innovative — and potentially lucrative — concepts in the revival in American brewing are brewpubs.

A brewpub is a restaurant or tavern which brews on the premises and sells to customers without bottling or distributing to other outlets (there are exceptions with a few brewpubs bottling small quantities or distributing kegs to other restaurants). Brewpubs were once very common in America before the 20th century when taverns brewed their own beer and sold to customers and other taverns that didn't brew.

AMERICA'S FIRST MODERN BREWPUB

The first brewpub in the American microbrewing revolution was the Yakima Brewing and Malting Company in Yakima, Washington, begun by Bert Grant in the summer of 1982. Grant had been involved in brewing for 40 years as a brewing chemist with various Canadian breweries, research director at Stroh and technical director at S. S. Steiner, a producer of hops from the Yakima Valley.

Grant opened his brewpub in an abandoned opera house in downtown Yakima; his first beer was Grant's Scottish Ale, a nut-brown ale brewed with Yakima Valley Cascade hops.

BREWPUBS MIGRATE TO CALIFORNIA

The Northwest brewpub concept quickly migrated to California when entrepreneurial-minded homebrewers like Bill Owens (Buffalo Bill's Microbrewery; Hayward) persuaded legislators to amend the law and

permit a small-scale brewery to retail beer in California without a distributor. The Mendocino Brewing Company in tiny Hopland, two hours
north of San Francisco, became California's first brewpub when it opened
in August 1983. The brewery used equipment from the old New Albion
brewery and made English-style ales to sell to local customers who tended
to be laid-back California farmers, marijuana growers, loggers and tourists
heading up Highway 101.

A month later, former award-winning photographer Bill Owens
opened his brewpub south of San Francisco in a working class neighborhood in the East Bay community of Hayward. Owens brewed "Buffalo
Bill lager" from a recipe he had developed during his 15 years as a
homebrewer.

The California media fell in love with the local brewpubs and featured
them in articles, radio and TV reports. The media attention did nothing
to hurt sales and today, both brewpubs are prospering and planning to
expand.

The Hopland and Hayward brewpubs inspired other California entrepreneurs and homebrewers intrigued with the concept. Within three
years, brewpubs opened in Berkeley, San Francisco, Petaluma and Santa
Cruz with others scheduled to open in 1987 in Oakland, Walnut Hills,
Sacramento and Los Angeles.

Following Bert Grant's introduction of brewpubs to the Northwest
in 1982, several others opened in British Columbia, Seattle and Portland.
By 1985, brewpubs had moved eastward, opening in New York (New
Amsterdam Brewery and Taproom and the Manhattan Brewery) and
Wisconsin (Hibernia, Eau Claire). In 1986, the Commonwealth brewpub
opened in Boston and the Weeping Radish restaurant began brewing in
Manteo, North Carolina.

BREWPUBS OFFER DIVERSITY
ALONG WITH CHARM

An interesting feature of brewpubs is that they allow for a great
range of diversity and charm. Current brewpubs run all the way from a
modern Manhattan saloon (New Amsterdam Brewery and Taproom), a
German beer garden (Hibernia), campus tavern (Roaring Rock, Berkeley)
to a local tavern chain (Hillsdale Brewery and several taverns owned by
Michael McMenamin, Portland).

Brewing beer on the premises is the only thing brewpubs have to
have in common; the rest of the operation, including theme, food and
atmosphere can be as traditional, trendy or funky as the owner desires.

The only limits are those of his imagination. For that reason alone, there is no reason there can't be hundreds of brewpubs in America, each as different as there are different bars or taverns.

THE FUTURE OF BREWPUBS

The future for brewpubs is virtually unlimited in both America and Canada; the challenge is to tap into the "upwardly mobile" food and drink conscious customers who want quality and authenticity in their food and entertainment. There are few cities in either America or Canada that wouldn't welcome a neighborhood brewpub that brews its own beer. It's only a matter of time before a major restaurant chain experiments with brewpubs and if the success of the first brewpubs are any indication, nationwide chains of brewpubs are only a few years away.

The start-up costs for a microbrewery run as high as $1 - $2 million and that's before a single bottle or keg is sold. A restaurant or tavern, on the other hand, in a state which permits brewpubs can install brewing equipment (after local zoning and health department approval, of course, and the necessary space for the equipment) for approximately $100-300,000 and begin selling beer within a couple of months.

One major commercial advantage that brewpubs have over micro-breweries is that they do not have the bottling, distribution and marketing problems that come with selling beer away from the brewery. For that reason alone, the number of brewpubs in North America will likely far exceed the number of microbreweries within the next decade. A town of a half million population is probably too small for a microbrewery to be very successful; that same town, however, could support several small brewpubs.

CALIFORNIA

BUFFALO BILL'S MICROBREWERY AND BREWPUB
1082 "B" Street
Hayward, California 94541
   (415) 886-9823

President/Brewmaster: William E. Owens
Founded: 1983
1985 Production: 450 barrels

"Buffalo Bill" Owens is one of the leaders of the brewpub movement in the U.S. A former award-winning photographer, Owens turned a 15 year homebrewing avocation into one of the first brewpubs in America when he opened Buffalo Bill's in September 1983, one month after the Hopland brewpub opened.

Bill does almost everything in his brewpub including brewing, sweeping up, tending bar, ordering supplies and giving tours of his brewery. He brews 180 gallons of his beer every Monday and invites customers into the back to observe. Standing on a ladder, Owens stirs his brew with a canoe paddle and describes how his beer is made.

Owens is both a brewer and microbrewing zealot. He is raising $300,000 to open another brewpub in the Bay Area and says, "In 10 years you'll be able to drive from San Diego to Eureka and never be more than a few minutes from a brewpub."

In a somewhat controversial step, Owens petitioned to trademark the term "brewpub" for his exclusive use in California. He has also applied for a federal trademark for the term. Owens believes, as do many others in the microbrewing movement, that brewpubs eventually will be franchised by large restaurant chains.

Owens was once visited by a representative of Suntory, the gigantic Japanese distilling and brewing corporation. The representative was interested in learning about the brewpub's operations and taking some pictures. Owens politely refused.

Owens also publishes *Amateur Brewer* magazine.

Buffalo Bill Lager — *the sole product brewed is Owens' own recipe: 300 pounds of six-row barley and three pounds of Cascade hops. Owens brews for nine hours then lets the beer age one week before it is piped 62 feet to the bar.*

MENDOCINO BREWING COMPANY
13351 S. Highway 101
Hopland, California 95449
(707) 744-1015

Partners: Michael Laybourn, Norman Franks, John Scahill
Brewmasters: Don Barkley & Michael Lovett
Founded: August 14, 1983
1986 Production: 748 barrels

The Hopland Brewery has a place in history as California's first brewpub, opening its doors in 1983 a few months after the California legislature changed the law permitting a brewery to sell on the premises.

Hopland is located 90 miles north of San Francisco in the heart of the Mendocino County wine-growing region. The beautiful Russian River valley is the home to the hawks and herons which the brewery's ales are named after.

Mendocino County was once a center of Northern California's logging and hop-growing industries. The local economy now depends upon tourism, a few wineries and marijuana farms reportedly hidden in the mountains around the county.

The Hopland Brewery is housed in a 100-year-old brick building that once served as the local post office and later the Hop Vine Saloon (the backyard beer garden is shaded by trellised hop plants). The brewpub's walls are covered with the original ornamental stamped tin; the bar is blonde oak and brass reminiscent of 19th century saloons.

The backroom brewhouse once belonged to the New Albion Brewery; brewmasters Barkley and Lovett made the trip north from Sonoma along with New Albion's brewing equipment.

Mendocino bottles a small amount of their ales in 51-ounce champagne magnum bottles. "We sell the heaviest and most expensive six pack in the world," Laybourn says, "It weighs 42 pounds and costs $42."

Peregrine Pale Ale — *brewed with 100% pale malt and Cascade hops.*

Blue Heron Ale — *English-style bitter made with pale malt, Clusters and Cascade hops.*

Red Tail Ale — *pale malt, caramel malt, Clusters and Cascade hops.*

Black Hawk Stout — *dark, full bodied, slightly sweet made with roasted black malt, pale, caramel malt; Clusters and Cascade hops.*

ROARING ROCK BREWERY
1920 Shattuck Avenue
Berkeley, California 94704
   (415) 843-2739

President: Reid and John Martin
Founded: 1986
Brewmaster: Rich Warner

The Roaring Rock Brewery looks like any campus tavern near a major university. This tavern, however, brews beer and lets patrons view the brewmaster working through a glass partition.

Roaring Rock's brewing operation extends along a narrow corridor from the front of the brewpub to the rear where grain, hops and supplies are stored. The stainless steel equipment is also visible from the front window so passersby can watch the brewing from the sidewalk and smell the boiling mash.

The brewpub serves sandwiches and is expanding a small rooftop beer garden to accommodate more customers. The brewpub decor includes memorabilia from old American breweries.

According to 27-year-old manager Reid Martin, Roaring Rock's success was much greater than expected when it opened early in 1986; production doubled each month for the first four months of operation. The clientele includes an eclectic mixture of Berkeley students, tourists, pub crawlers and beer groupies who have heard about the brewpub in "The Peoples' Republic of Berkeley."

In the short time since it opened, Roaring Rock has developed almost a cult following in the Bay area. Stringent space limitations, however, limit the brewery from expanding at its present location.

Pinnacle Pale Ale — *amber ale with mild hoppy flavor.*

Red Rock Ale — *a coppery red ale.*

Black Rock Porter — *a dark, medium heavy ale with slightly roasted flavor.*

★　　★　　★

REDWOOD BREWING COMPANY
21 Washington St.
Petaluma, California
   (707) 765-1445

President/Brewmaster: Jeff Berrington
Founded: 1985
1985 Production: 208 barrels

The Redwood Brewing opened in the fall of 1985 from a modest storefront in downtown Petaluma. The founder raised approximately $150,000 from family real estate holdings to open the brewpub.

Redwood brews one beer, Barbary Ale.

★   ★   ★

SAN FRANCISCO BREWING COMPANY
155 Columbus Avenue
San Francisco, California
   (415) 434-3344

Manager: Allen Paul
Founded: 1986

San Francisco's first brewpub is in a turn-of-the-century bar called The Albatross which dates back to 1904. Mayor Dianne Feinstein attended the grand opening.

Allen Paul is a former homebrewer who raised $400,000 to start his brewpub which was featured in a February 1987 *Newsweek* article.

★   ★   ★

SANTA CRUZ BREWING COMPANY
516 Front Street
Santa Cruz, California 95060
(408) 429-8838

Manager: Gerry Turgeon
Brewer: Scotty Morgan
Founded: 1986

The Front Street Brewpub, like Berkeley's Roaring Rock, opened in the spring of 1986; both are near the campus of major California universities (Berkeley and Santa Cruz State).

Manager Gerry Turgeon said the brewery reached the first year's production level of 1,000 barrels a week six days after it opened. The brewery also makes root beer from dandelion root, sarsaparilla, wintergreen, juniper berries and sugar.

The brewpub menu includes burgers, seafood, steamed mussels, clams and pot pies. A specialty of the house is "speedies," charbroiled spicy pork on skewers.

★   ★   ★

HOG'S HEAD
114 J St.
Sacramento, California
(916) 443-2739

★   ★   ★

TRUCKEE BREWING COMPANY
P.O. BOX 2615
Truckee, California 95734
(916) 587-7411

★   ★   ★

MASSACHUSETTS

COMMONWEALTH BREWING COMPANY
85 Merrimac Street
Boston, Massachusetts 02114
    (617) 523-8383

President: Richard Wrigley
Brewmaster: Phil Leinhart
Founded: 1986

Richard Wrigley left the Manhattan Brewing Company in 1985 after helping to launch New York's first brewpub. He moved to Boston convinced that Massachusetts, once the home to many ale breweries, was ready for a locally-brewed ale once again. Commonwealth is Massachusetts only operating brewery and the first brewery in Boston since the Haffenreffer Brewery closed 20 years ago.

Commonwealth's two-story brewpub resembles a busy English pub near London's financial district. The brewpub's brewing equipment is visible through glass walls on both floors with the decorative 200-gallon copper brewkettles the centerpiece. Customers have a choice of drinking standing at the bar, at upended beer barrels that serve as tables, or seated at long copper-covered tables.

All of Commonwealth's beers are highly hopped English-style ales with little carbonation. Five ales are on tap at all times including specials such as Boston's Best Burton Bitter, Winter Warmer, Ginger Ale and Massachusetts Ale. The ales are drawn from casks by English hand pumps which don't require carbonation to move the beer. Wrigley has persuaded several farmers to grow experimental hops and barley to make all-Massachusetts beer.

Wrigley's next venture is to open brewpubs in New Orleans and San Francisco.

★   ★   ★

NEW YORK

MANHATTAN BREWING COMPANY
40-42 Thompson Street
New York, New York 10013
    (212) 219-9250

President: Robert J. D'Addona
Brewmaster: Mark Witty
Founded: 1985
1986 Production: 4,000 barrels

The former Consolidated Edison Thompson Street substation is the home of Manhattan's first brewery since the Ruppert Brewery shut its doors in 1965. It took two years and more than $1 million to turn the substation — which had no gas, electricity, roof and holes in the floor — into a working brewpub.

The brewpub has two restaurants, the first-floor Tap Room and second-floor Ocean Grill with different menus featuring pub food or regular dinners.

The showpiece of the brewpub are the Tap Room's decorative copper brewkettles. Brewing, however, is done on the third floor since the weight of the copper kettles filled with beer would send them crashing through the floor if brewing were ever attempted. Several English-style ales, porters and stouts are brewed.

Behind the brewery is a small stable where two English shire horses, Prince and Duke, are kept. The horses draw the beer wagon during parades and occasionally deliver beer to SoHo taverns and restaurants.

Royal Amber — *the brewery claims this ale is made from George Washington's recipe.*

★　★　★

NEW AMSTERDAM BREWERY AND TAPROOM
1045 45th St.
New York, New York 10001
    (212) 255-4100

President: Matthew Reich
Brewmaster: Dr. Joseph Owades
Founded: 1985
1986 Production: 9,000 barrels

The New Amsterdam Brewery and Taproom is a classic American saloon that Matthew Reich designed for upscale and trend-conscious New Yorkers. Reich chose a converted railroad warehouse in the Chelsea section of Manhattan so that customers could see brewery's equipment while having lunch and dinner and later take a tour of the brewery.

The Taproom has high ceilings and is decorated with posters from early American breweries. A blonde-wood bar separates the restaurant from the brewery with two working copper brewkettles behind the bar.

New Amsterdam Amber Beer
(See microbrewing directory)

★   ★   ★

NORTH CAROLINA

WEEPING RADISH
P.O. Box 1471
Manteo, North Carolina 27954
(919) 473-1157

President: Edward Greene
Brewmaster: Karl Lechner
Founded: 1986

Edward Greene owned the highly successful "Island Art Gallery and Christmas Shop" in Manteo but wanted to open a German-style restaurant for the tourists who visit North Carolina's Outer Banks and nearby Cape Hatteras every year.

Greene visited Bavaria and returned with the idea that a small brewery in his restaurant would be successful. He worked to change the law in North Carolina and opened his brewpub on July 4, 1986. The Weeping Radish is North Carolina's first brewpub and the only German-style brewpub in America.

The Weeping Radish is a Bavarian restaurant that imports all its food from Germany. German chef Edward Eck prepares potato soup, wiener schnitzel, cordon bleu, sausages and many German specialty dishes. Brewmaster Karl Lechner was brought over from the Hopf brewery in Miesback and worked with fellow-German brewer Wolfgang Roth of the Chesapeake Brewing Company during the brewery start-up.

The name Weeping Radish refers to a German radish served with beer in Bavarian restaurants. When sliced, spiraled, salted and put back together, moisture beads from the radish as if it were "weeping."

Hopf Weisser Bock — A light German-style lager.

OREGON

PORTLAND BREWING COMPANY
1339 Northwest Flanders Street
Portland, Oregon 97209
   (503) 222-7150

Partners: Fred Bowman and Art Larrance
Brewer: Frank Commanday
Founded: 1986

The inspiration for the Portland Brewery came from two businessmen who saw a good idea and wanted to capitalize on it. Fred Bowman and Art Larrance had extensive real estate and business experience in Portland and had seen Northwest microbreweries and brewpubs start up in the early 1980s. They felt the brewpub trend was in its infancy and wanted to jump in -- even if they knew nothing about brewing.

To get over this small hurdle, Bowman and Larrance struck a consulting agreement with Yakima's Bert Grant who started America's first brewpub in 1982. Grant agreed to help Bowman and Larrance and designed their brewpub; in return, Bowman and Larrance brew and sell Grant's beer under license.

Not surprisingly, there is a similarity between the two brewpubs. Both have an English pub atmosphere (Grant's Yakima operation is more authentic) complete with pub food and dart boards.

Portland Brewing is in a revitalized neighborhood where taverns, galleries and boutiques are breathing new life into a once dying area of Portland. The Widmer Brewery, Blitz Weinhard and the Columbia River Brewery (another brewpub) are a couple of blocks away.

A wonderful tradition has been revived by the Portland Brewery — selling "beer by the bucket" as American saloons used to do earlier in this century. For $5, customers can buy a plastic bucket with 60 ounces of fresh beer. Customers frequently stop by to pick up a bucket of fresh ale on their home from work. A delightful custom!

Portland Ale — *a pale ale made from hops from Oregon (Nugget) and Washington (Cascade).*

★   ★   ★

COLUMBIA RIVER BREWING COMPANY
(BRIDGEPORT PUBLIC HOUSE)
1313 N.W. Marshall
Portland, Oregon 97209
(503) 241-7179

Founder: Dick Ponzi
Brewers: Karl Ockert and Matt Sage
Founded: 1984
1986 Production: 2,000 barrels

Columbia River Brewing is Oregon's first microbrewery. It is located in Portland's oldest industrial building (1886) in a revitalized area around the corner from the Widmer Brewery and a few blocks from the Blitz-Weinhard Brewery and Portland Brewing brewpub.

Ivy covering the front of the building conveys an historical authenticity to the brewery. The brewpub has an outdoor patio on an old loading dock where customers sit when weather permits in rainy Portland.

Columbia River began brewing ales and stouts for Portland taverns and restaurants in 1984 before its brewpub opened early in 1986. The atmosphere in the brewpub is casual and has a rustic charm to it.

Bridgeport's "publican" (an English bartender, although our word conveys little of the character endowed by the English term) is Scot Stuart Ramsay, who is pleasantly chatty and hospitable to customers.

BridgePort Ale — *the original ale brewed in 1984; an English-style brownish ale brewed with pale two-row and dark caramel malt; Washington Clusters, Oregon Willamette and British Columbia Chilliwack hops.*

BridgePort Stout — *brewed with pale, caramel and black patent malt and similar combination of hops as BridgePort Ale; rich black color.*

BridgePort Golden Ale — *honey colored, light, crisp and hoppy; similar to English bitter.*

Paddy's Special Red Ale; Rose City Ale; Old Knucklehead Barley-wine — *specialty ales brewed for different seasons*

★   ★   ★

HILLSDALE BREWERY AND PUBLIC HOUSE
1505 S. W. Sunset Blvd.
Portland, Oregon 97201
    (503) 246-3938

President: R.W. McMenamin
Brewer: Mike McMenamin/Conrad Santos
Founded: 1985

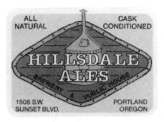

Portland has the distinction of having the most breweries (seven) of any city in America. Three of them are brewpubs owned by Mike McMenamin, a local tavern entrepreneur. McMenamin brews at his three brewpubs (Hillsdale, Portland; Lighthouse, Lincoln City; and Cornelius Pass Roadhouse, Hillsboro) and distributes beer to his other three Portland-area taverns. Oregon law permits three brewpubs per brewing permit.

The brewing operation at the Hillsdale Brewery is inside "Captain Neon's Fermentation Chamber," a garish backroom complete with flashing neon lights and Day-Glo colors reminiscent of another Oregonian, Ken Kesey of Merry Pranksters fame.

McMenamin uses malt extract to brew his ales and includes an assortment of non-traditional brewing ingredients such as blackberries, cinnamon, cloves, nutmeg and even Mars candy bars. The names for his ales are just as colorful: Terminator, Hammerhead, Ruby Tuesday, Kris Kringle and Mars Ales.

★   ★   ★

WASHINGTON

YAKIMA BREWING & MALTING COMPANY
25 North Front Street
Yakima, Washington 98901
    (509) 575-1900

President/Brewmaster: Bert Grant
Founded: 1982
1985 production: 4,000 barrels

The Switzer Opera House in downtown Yakima is the home of America's first brew-pub, Yakima Brewing & Malting Company. Bert Grant, a revered figure in American brewing, is the founder, brewmaster, and guiding force behind this establishment.

Yakima ales are distributed throughout the Northwest; in Seattle alone, more than 50 taverns and restaurants carry Grant's Scottish Ale, Apple Cider and Imperial Stout.

Grant has worked in the brewing industry for 40 years and today is the technical director for S. S. Steiner, a Yakima hop grower. The Yakima Valley is one of the world's largest hop growing regions and all ales brewed by Grant use locally grown hops.

Grant's brewpub serves English style "pub-grub" such as bangers (sausages), sausage rolls, and ploughman's lunch.

At the 1984 Great American Beer Festival, Grant's Imperial Stout won the top prize for American beers; his Scottish Ale was runner-up. Yakima's brewhouse is next door to the brewpub and the cooling room is inside the vault of the old opera house.

India Pale Ale — *brewed with Klages pale malt and more than one pound of Eroica and Galena hops per barrel.*

Imperial Stout — *at 8% alcohol, one of the strongest draft beers in the U.S. Honey is added for the additional alcohol.*

Scottish Ale — *amber ale with a slight caramel taste, brewed with Cascade hops.*

Christmas Ale — *brewed between Thanksgiving and New Years with a mixture of honey, cinnamon, ginger and nutmeg.*

Celtic Ale — *brewed with three malts and Cascade hops.*

Yakima Hard Cider — *the only draught hard cider in the country.*

WISCONSIN

WALTER PARK (HIBERNIA BREWING COMPANY)
318 Elm Street
Eau Claire, Wisconsin 54703
  (715) 836-2336

President: Michael Healy
Brewer: John Walter
Founded: 1985

When Michael Healy was going over the paperwork to purchase the 95-year-old Walter Brewery in Eau Claire, he discovered that an adjacent vacant one-acre parcel of land was owned by the brewery. Like most old breweries, Walter's at one time had an outdoor beer garden for employees and their families.

Shortly after Healy started to operate his new brewery, he cleaned up the vacant lot, turned it into a beer garden and named it after the founder of the original brewery.

Healy cultivates a family atmosphere at Walter Park, which is located in a working-class neighborhood of Eau Claire. Every night during the summer, customers sit at picnic tables and stroll around the grassy, wooded park to talk with neighbors and friends. Country and western singers, German polka bands, bluegrass and jazz groups play on the weekends.

The park is open daily (weather permitting) from noon until 11:00 PM with a "happy hour" Monday-Thursday. Light sandwiches, salads, pizza are served with pitchers of Hibernia and Walter beers and soft drinks made at the brewery.

★   ★   ★

FUTURE BREWPUBS

CALIFORNIA

BUSTER'S
Buena Park, California
(714) 521-7903

COLZAXX'S CASTLE
Chico, California

DEVIL MOUNTAIN BREWERY
Walnut Creek, California 94596
(415) 935-2337

KENTUCKY

OLD HEIDELBERG
Fort Mitchell, Kentucky 41017
(606) 341-2800

MASSACHUSETTS

NORTHAMPTON BREWERY/BREWSTER COURT PUB
Northampton, Massachusetts 01060
(413) 584-9903

NEW YORK

BUFFALO BREWPUB
Williamsville, New York 14221
(716) 632-0552

PENNSYLVANIA

STOUDT BREWERY
Adamstown, Pennsylvania 19501
(215) 484-4385

VIRGINIA

BLUE RIDGE MOUNTAIN BREWERY
Charlottesville, Virginia 22901
(804) 977-0017

WISCONSIN

THE BREWMASTERS PUB
Kenosha, Wisconsin 53142
(414) 694-9050

CANADIAN MICROBREWERIES AND BREWPUBS

The American microbrewing revolution is being duplicated north of the 39th parallel in Canada. And, as might be expected of two friendly neighbors who share a common language (with the exception of Quebec), there are many parallels between the American and Canadian movements.

The Canadian brewing scene before the 1980s was much like the American; mergers and consolidations had led to a virtual monopoly in the marketplace by "industrial breweries." In the case of Canada, those breweries were Labatts, Molson and Carling O'Keefe.

With a dwindling choice of beers and beer styles, Canadians began homebrewing in the 1970s. And, as could be expected, the first Canadian microbrewers were former homebrewers.

Geography and regionalism also was a factor in the early days of Canadian microbrewing. Like their American counterparts, Canadian microbreweries started on the West Coast and moved eastward.

BRITISH COLUMBIA:
HOME OF FIRST CANADIAN MICROBREWERIES
AND BREWPUBS

Canadians look to British Columbia (actually the cities of Vancouver and Victoria) as a trend setting province much like Americans consider California (and San Francisco and Los Angeles) as the state where cultural trends begin.

As one commentator said on Canadian Broadcasting Corporation (CBC), the national radio network, "If you want to know what is going to be hot in Toronto or Montreal next year, find out what's happening in Vancouver this year. And there's a good chance that what's popular today in Vancouver probably started in San Francisco a year or two ago."

That analysis applies with the microbrewing revolution. The first microbreweries and brewpubs started in British Columbia in the early 1980s and have recently moved eastward into the provinces of Alberta, Manitoba, Ontario, Quebec and even Nova Scotia and Prince Edward Island.

Just as there are models of successful American microbreweries, two operations have emerged as leaders in Canada: Granville Island, a $2 million Vancouver microbrewery, and Spinnakers brewpub in Victoria.

Both Granville Island and Spinnakers started in 1984, the same year that saw 17 microbreweries and brewpubs open in the U.S. — including a half-dozen in the Seattle-Portland corridor south of British Columbia.

That hallowed "community of brewers" attitude exists between North American microbreweries. Because U.S. micros had a two or three year head start, most Canadian pioneering microbrewers made the trek to Washington, Oregon and California before taking the plunge. The Canadians found the Americans helpful and supportive in their efforts to export microbrewing north of the border. Now there are so many Canadian microbreweries — especially in British Columbia — that Canadians need not venture south to see successful microbreweries and brewpubs. Nevertheless, many still do.

FIRST INTERNATIONAL CONTRACT BREWING ARRANGEMENT: GRANVILLE ISLAND BREWS FOR PASADENA

The "community of brewers" relationship took an interesting turn late in 1986 when the Granville Island Brewery in Vancouver began exporting contract-brewed beer south of the border for the new Pasadena Brewing Company which opened in December. This is the first "international contract brewing" arrangement that has been set up and if it is successful, more international deals may be struck in the future between American and Canadian microbreweries.

According to the Pasadena brewery, the Granville Island beer is brewed and bottled on a Friday and driven by truck over the weekend so that the beer will arrive Monday morning for immediate delivery to Pasadena's local accounts.

This deal between Granville Island and Pasadena was consummated in time for Pasadena to be declared the "unofficial beer" of the 1987 Super Bowl held in Pasadena on January 25.

CANADIAN MICROS EXPAND EASTWARD

Canadian microbreweries appear to be growing in popularity as rapidly as American microbreweries. Here again, the two countries demographics largely determine where microbreweries have the best chance of succeeding. The West Coast (in both Canada and the U.S.) remains the most fertile area for microbreweries to emerge in next few years, with several ventures in East Coast urban areas (Montreal, Toronto, Quebec; New York, Boston, Philadelphia and Washington) moving aggressively to take advantage of consumer interest and large markets.

New microbrewing ventures are currently underway in Ontario: two breweries in Ottawa (Montferrand Brewing and Ottawa Valley Brewing), another in Windsor (Ambassador Brewing) and brewpubs in Ft. Erie (Shackles Restaurant), Toronto (Queen's Quay Restaurant) and Kingston (Clearance House Restaurant).

It is in East Coast population centers in both nations that microbreweries could realize their greatest potential as alternatives to industrial breweries. But microbreweries don't only exist on the East or West Coast; there are several in the Midwest heartland (Wisconsin, Minnesota, Manitoba and Ontario) where there is a history of small breweries. The large population of northern Europeans (particularly Germans and Scandinavians) are part of the reason for the emergence of microbreweries in these states and provinces.

ALBERTA

THE PACIFIC AVENUE BREWPUB
213 10th Avenue, S.W.
Calgary, Alberta T2R OA4
  (403) 234-7754

Founder: Bruce Plance
Founded: 1985

In June 1985, the three Plance brothers (Dave, Don and Bruce) started Alberta's first brewpub. The Plances' father is the agricultural minister for Alberta. Their operation is a turn-key brewery manufactured by Cask Brewing, Ltd. of Vancouver.

The brewpub occupies two floors in a downtown location near shops, restaurants and office buildings. Upstairs is a traditional saloon serving lunch and dinner with jukebox music at night; the downstairs bar caters to the sports-minded with giant TV screens for watching football, hockey and baseball. The basement brewery is visible to customers at the entrance of the brewpub.

The Pacific Avenue brewpub uses malt extract to brew its Livingston Lager (named after an Alberta pioneer) and Smart Ale (named after a local fire chief).

★   ★   ★

BOCCALINO PASTA BISTRO AND BREWPUB
Edmonton, Alberta

President: Peter Johner
Founded: 1986

★   ★   ★

STRATHCONA BREWING COMPANY
4914-A 89th St.
Edmonton, Alberta T6E SK1
  (403) 465-0553

President: Robert Herscovitch
Founded: 1986

★   ★   ★

BRITISH COLUMBIA

GRANVILLE ISLAND BREWING
1441 Cartwright Street
Granville Island
Vancouver, British Columbia V6H 3R7
   (604) 668-9927

President: Mitch Taylor
Brewmaster: Rainer Kallahne
Founded: 1984

Granville Island is the first microbrewery in Canada. It bottles two lager beers in a restored warehouse near the Expo 86 site along the Vancouver waterfront. The building is an art deco structure which is contrasted by the modern, stainless steel brewery equipment inside. The founders raised $2.5 million with a limited partnership to build their showcase brewery.

Many consider Granville Island a leader in the Canadian microbrewing movement because of the quality of its beer and the design of the brewery. The partners purchased top-of-the line equipment, hired a German-educated brewer, built an impressive facility and generally took few short cuts in establishing a first-rate brewery and brewing high quality beer.

Visitors can purchase beer at a retail outlet inside the brewery. From the outlet and the taproom next door, visitors can view the brewhouse and bottling line. A kegging line will be added to serve Vancouver's restaurants and pubs.

Granville Island recently went public and is expanding production to brew 17,000 barrels per year.

Late in 1986, Granville Island began contract brewing for the new Pasadena Brewing Company in California in the first international brewing agreement between Canadian and American microbreweries.

Island Lager — *brewed with Canadian pale malt, German Hallertauer and Spalt hops.*

Island Bock — *a reddish color beer full in body and similar to a German doppelbock.*

★   ★   ★

ISLAND PACIFIC BREWING
24-6809 Kirkpatrick Crescent, R.R. 3
Victoria, British Columbia V8X 3X1
(604) 652-4722

President: John Hellemond
Brewmaster: Hermann Hoerterer
Founded: 1985

After some start-up difficulties and problems with the quality of beer, Island Pacific has become a popular draft beer in British Columbia. Part of the turn-around was the hiring of German brewer Hermann Hoerterer who instituted quality control standards and a more efficient kegging operation.

Island Pacific has been aggressively pursuing new accounts in British Columbia since the provincial law was changed to permit restaurants to carry draft beer. The brewery is producing small keg coolers to install in pubs or restaurants with limited space and has purchased a Sankey kegging line which empties, sterilizes, fills, and closes kegs in seconds. These kegs can be tapped easily in restaurants with simple instructions.

Island Pacific uses a food service wholesaler to distribute around British Columbia. A bottling line is planned to expand marketing opportunities throughout the province.

Goldstream Lager — *light, pale gold lager made from Canadian two-row malt; Yakima Clusters and Cascade hops.*

Key Lager — *uses combination of pale, caramel and black malts; Cascade and Hallertauer hops.*

Hermann's No. 1 Bavarian Dark — *named after brewer Hermann Hoerterer; brewed with Munich, caramel and black malts and imported Perle, Hallertauer and Saaz hops. Although produced in limited quantities, Hermann's No. 1 has developed a passionate following in British Columbia.*

★   ★   ★

BRYANT'S BREWERY
22720 Dewdney Trunk Road
Maple Ridge, British Columbia V2X 3K3
    (604) 463-3545

Brewmaster: Paul Haupenthal
Founded: 1983

This small brewery reportedly has only three accounts in pubs in the eastern Vancouver suburbs. Two beers (Bullfrog Bitter and Bryant's Lager) are brewed.

A small tasting room in the brewery serves beer to visitors. The brewery's founder, Peter Bryant, sold it to Mistral Resources in 1984.

★   ★   ★

MOUNTAIN ALES
13130 88th Avenue
Surrey, British Columbia V3W 3K3
    (604) 591-1211

President: Ralph Berezan
Brewmaster: Geoff Boraston
Founded: 1983

The Mountain Ales brewery was built by Frank Appleton, a brewing consultant from British Columbia who helped launch the Horseshoe Bay Brewery, Spinnakers and Island Pacific. A series of production and marketing problems has plagued the brewery since it opened and it is reportedly for sale.

Two British style ales (Mountain Malt and Mountain Premium Ale) are brewed.

★   ★   ★

NORTH ISLAND BREWING
1364 Spruce Street
Campbell River, British Columbia V9W 5T4
(604) 286-1822

President: Dennis Berston
Brewmaster: Erik Mairs
Founded: 1986

The North Island Brewery is one of the newest microbreweries in British Columbia, having opened in the spring of 1986. The brewery bottles and kegs West Coast Tug Lager made from Canadian pale two-row malt, black patent malt and Cascade hops.

★　★　★

OKANAGAN SPRING BREWING
2801 27A Avenue
Vernon, British Columbia V1T 8C3
(604) 542-2337

President: Jacob Tobler
Brewmaster: Raimund Kalinowski
Founded: 1985

The Okanagan Valley is a fertile agricultural region well-known for its orchards, wineries, and ski resorts. The Okanagan Spring Brewery is located in a warehouse previously used to store apples. This is British Columbia's first inland brewery, located approximately a six-hour drive from Vancouver.

Two lager beers (Okanagan Spring Premium Lager and Okanagan Spring Bavarian Light) are brewed in the modern facility. Both German-style lager beers use Canadian two-row malt and German Hallertauer hops.

Brewer Kalinowski was a classmate at the University of Berlin Brewing School of Rainer Kallahne, brewer at Granville Island in Vancouver.

★　★　★

STEVESTON BREWING COMPANY
Steveston, British Columbia

President: Frank Malek
Founded: 1986

This small brewery began brewing 4,000 cases per week in July 1986 when it opened. Three brews (Steveston Heritage Pilsner, Steveston Heritage Pilsner Light and Steveston Heritage Ale) are produced and sold in the Vancouver area.

★ ★ ★

BREWPUBS
BRITISH COLUMBIA

SPINNAKERS BREWPUB (VICTORIA WEST BREWERY)
308 Catherine Street
Victoria, British Columbia V9A 3S8
   (604) 384-6613

President: Paul Elliot
Brewmaster: Brad McQuhue
Founded: 1984

Since Spinnakers opened in May 1984, it has become legendary in the Northwest for its beers and nautical ambiance.

Spinnakers was started by John Mitchell who earlier opened the Horseshoe Bay brewery. But in September 1986, Mitchell stepped aside, turning over his interest in the brewpub to his partners. Mitchell had reportedly "burned out" after struggling for two years with B.C. liquor board authorities on various legal issues involving the operation and expansion of Spinnakers.

Spinnakers' owners vow to continue their plans to expand the brewpub which is located in the West Victoria harbor destined for commercial growth in the near future. They are hoping to convince provincial authorities that the current 65-seat limit for the brewpub be increased. An upstairs dining room is all but ready to open as soon as the seating limitation dilemma is resolved with B.C. liquor officials.

Spinnakers fans are legendary in Victoria. When ships and ferries leave port, ship captains — many of whom are loyal Spinnakers customers — blow the ship's horn when sailing past the brewpub. Customers inside Spinnakers raise their glasses in a toast for a safe return to the brewpub.

Spinnakers is clean and modern with natural light streaming in from floor-to-ceiling windows facing the harbor. Pictures of nautical scenes and old Canadian breweries adorn the walls. The casual atmosphere is similar to what one might find in an English neighborhood pub.

Spinnakers brews a variety of ales and lagers depending upon the season. Four brews (Spinnaker Ale, Mitchell's Extra Special Bitter, Mt. Tolmie Dark Ale, Empress Stout, Ogden Porter, Genoa Lager and Christmas Ale) are carried at one time at the brewpub's taps. The beer is dispensed via British "beer engines" which pulls the beer from casks in the basement.

Spinnakers' menu is simple but bountiful; light salads, hamburgers and fresh seafood are specialties.

CELLAR BREWERY
Terminal Hotel
Nanaimo, British Columbia V9R 5B9
(604) 754-4323

President: Patrick O'Keefe
Founded: 1984

In the fall of 1986, the hotel and brewery were being sold. The brewery used malt extract in its brews.

★ ★ ★

HORSESHOE BAY BREWERY/TROLLER PUB
6695 Nelson Avenue
Horseshoe Bay, British Columbia V7W 2H2
(604) 921-8310

President: David Patrick
Brewmaster: David Bruce-Thomas
Founded: 1982

The Troller Pub became the first North American brewpub when it opened in June 1982. Troller's also has the distinction of brewing the first cask-conditioned ale in North America. Its founder, John Mitchell, later moved to Victoria to open Spinnakers brewpub.

The small brewery is located in a warehouse a couple hundred yards from the brewpub (B.C. provincial law in 1982 required a brewery and retail operation to be in separate facilities). Troller's brewpub is the only outlet for the Horseshoe Brewery.

Horseshoe's English-style ales (Bay Ale, Royal Ale, Pale Ale) are brewed with English pale malt and a variety of Canadian (Chilliwack), American (Cascade), German (Hallertauer) and English hops (Kent Goldings).

★ ★ ★

THE LEEWARD
649 Anderton Road
Comox, British Columbia
  (604) 339-5400

President: Gil Gaudry
Founded: 1984

Brews Leeward Lager and a light ale from malt extract.

★   ★   ★

THE PRAIRIE INN
7806 E. Saanich Road
Saanichton, British Columbia V0S 1M0
  (604) 652-1575

President: Ted Anderson
Founded: 1983

The Prairie Inn is a popular, English-style neighborhood pub that draws a mixture of locals, tourists, and visitors from Victoria. It is in a large public house with overflowing flowerpots, an outdoor patio, pool table and TV sports room complete with blackboard for posting sports bets.

The Inn changed hands in 1985 when local restaurateur Ted Anderson bought it with the intention of starting a chain of brewpubs in B.C. Anderson is in the process of opening a second brewpub along the waterfront in Victoria.

The Prairie Inn uses malt extracts for its brews.

★   ★   ★

NOVA SCOTIA

GINGER'S TAVERN
1268 Hollis Street
Halifax, Nova Scotia B3J 2L4
(902) 423-1395

President: Kevin Keefe
Founded: 1985

Ginger's is the first brewpub in the eastern provinces.

★ ★ ★

ONTARIO

THE BRICK BREWING COMPANY
181 S. King Street
Waterloo, Ontario N2J 1P7
(519) 576-9100

President: James Brickman
Founded: 1984

The first microbrewery in the eastern provinces.

★ ★ ★

CONNERS BREWING COMPANY, LTD.
1 First Canadian Place, Suite 2540
Toronto, Ontario M5X 1A9
(416) 366-9715

President: Bruce Parker
Founded: 1986

This microbrewery will be manufacturing turn-key systems for brewpubs and microbreweries.

★ ★ ★

UPPER CANADA BREWING COMPANY, LTD.
2 Atlantic Avenue
Toronto, Ontario M6K 1X8
    (416) 534-9281

President: Frank Heaps
Founded: 1985

★   ★   ★

WELLINGTON COUNTY BREWERY, LTD.
950 Woodlawn Rd. W.
Guelph, Ontario N1K 1B8
    (519) 837-2337

Managing Director: David Willis
Founded: 1985

The Wellington Brewery produces the only cask-conditioned ale in North America. Its ales are hopped with English Fuggles and East Kent Goldings hops.

★   ★   ★

ATLAS HOTEL
35 Southworth St. N.
Welland, Ontario C3B 1X8
    (416) 732-5054

President: Albert Coutu
Founded: 1986

The brewpub is part of a hotel and entertainment complex. The brewery uses malt extract.

★   ★   ★

KINGSTON BREWING COMPANY
34 Clarence St.
Kingston, Ontario K7Z 1W9
   (613) 542-4978

President: Richard Cilles
Founded: 1986

★   ★   ★

PRINCE EDWARD ISLAND

ISLAND BREWERY
P.O. Box 1177
Charlottetown, Prince Edward Island C1A 7MB
   (902) 566-4200

President: William Rix, Jr.
Founded: 1986

★   ★   ★

QUEBEC

MASSAWIPPI BREWING COMPANY, INC.
55 Main, Box 568
North Hatley, Quebec J0B 2C0
   (819) 842-4259

President: Don Fleischer
Founded: 1986

★   ★   ★

FAMOUS DATES
IN BREWING

6000 B.C.   Mesopotamian clay tablets describe brewing.

4000 B.C.   Egyptians brew beer as common beverage; Pyramid builders drink beer during construction.

2000 B.C   King Hammurabi of Babylon writes laws about selling and brewing beer.

1000 B.C.   Finnish saga, Kalevala, describes brewing.

1215   King John signs Magna Carta; ale used as unit of weight.

1492   Columbus discovers Indians drinking fermented beverage made from corn and maize.

1500   Spanish and Portuguese explorers find Indians drinking "pulque" made from fermented corn.

1516   Reinheitsgebot purity law written by Bavarian king; allows only malted barley, hops and water for brewing beer in Germany.

1556   Use of hops in brewing legalized in England.

1620   Mayflower beer provisions run low; Pilgrims land at Plymouth, Massachusetts instead of Virginia.

1622   Peter Minuit opens first North American pub on Manhattan Island.

1630   First commercial brewery in the New World begun in Charleston, part of old Boston.

1632   Dutch set up first commercial brewery in New Amsterdam (New York) on "Brouwers (Brewers) Straet."

1639   First President of Harvard, Nathanial Easton, dismissed partly because he couldn't provide beer ration to students.

1720   English publicans "invent" porter, blend of ale and stout.

1770s   George Washington, Thomas Jefferson, James Madison, Patrick Henry, Samuel Adams and Benjamin Franklin involved in ale brewing.

1775   Dr. Benjamin Rush, future signer of the Declaration of Independence, publishes "An Inquiry into the Effects of Spirituous Liquors on the Human Body," which becomes the basic tract for the temperance movement.

1776   Declaration of Independence signed; Founding Fathers repair to Philadelphia pubs to celebrate by drinking ales.

1810   First census of breweries in America; Secretary of Treasury reports 132 breweries producing 185,000 barrels annually. Pennsylvania leads with 48 breweries; New York, 42; Ohio, 13.

                Jefferson becomes home brewer at Monticello after leaving Presidency; corresponds with home brewers James Madison and John Adams.

1814   Francis Scott Key writes "Star Spangled Banner" in a Baltimore pub, the Fountain Inn. Key uses tune from old English drinking song, "To Anacreon in Heaven."

1826   First temperance society formed calls for moderation in alcohol consumption but encourages drinking beer, wine, cider and malt liquor.

1836   American Temperance Union calls for abstinence.

1840   German immigrants Anheuser, Schaefer, Schlitz, Pabst, Busch come to U.S. and open breweries; lager beers and biergartens become way of life.

1849   California gold rush; breweries follow miners. Steam beer becomes popular in California.

1850	421 breweries in U.S.
1851	Maine passes first prohibition law in U.S.
1857	Eberhard Anheuser acquires brewery in St. Louis; Henry Weinhard establishes brewery in Portland.
1860	1,269 breweries in U.S. producing one million barrels of beer.
1862	Congress passes Internal Revenue Tax which levies $1/barrel tax on beer to pay for Civil War.
	First federation of brewers founded in U.S. (forerunner of present-day Beer Institute).
1867	3,700 breweries in U.S producing 6 million barrels/year; at least one brewery in every state.
1872	Prohibition becomes issue in Presidential election of Ulysses S. Grant.
1873	55% of tax collected under Internal Revenue Tax comes from breweries and distilleries.
	4,131 breweries in U.S., highest number ever reached; annual production of 9 million barrels.
1875	Pasteur discovers role of yeast in fermenting beer; publishes book, *On the Brewing of Beer*.
1876	Golden Age of Brewing in America. Centennial Exposition in Philadelphia; breweries build gigantic exhibit hall to display technological achievements of last 100 years.
1883	First pure lager yeast developed in Danish laboratory; Carlsberg Brewery in Copenhagen receives first strain.
1887	Pabst becomes first American brewery to use pure lager yeast for brewing.
1898	Tax on breweries pays for 40% of American involvement in the Spanish-American War.
1900	Carry Nation swings ax (as well as sledgehammer, rocks, bricks and iron bars) in her anti-saloon crusade.

1910	Mergers, consolidations lead to decline in number of breweries to 1,500 producing almost 60 million barrels/year; national breweries producing million barrels per year emerging.
1911	America becomes world leading producer of beer, brewing 62.8 million barrels; Germany No. 2 at 55 million barrels.
1912	Census figures record brewing as 25th largest industry employing 54,589 people with annual sales of $375 million.
1916	Temperance and anti-saloon legislation passed in 23 states.
1917	U.S. enters World War I; President Wilson limits alcohol content of beer to 2¾% by weight.
1919	18th Amendment passes calling for national prohibition.
1920	(January 16) Volstead Act takes effect, "Noble Experiment" begins; 2,000 breweries close their doors — most forever.
1920s	Speakeasies, gin mills, illegal stills and homebrewing flourish all over the country during Roaring '20s in defiance of nationwide prohibition. Gangsters Al Capone, Bugs Moran and Dutch Schultz run illegal breweries in Chicago and New York.
1921	U.S. Treasury estimate of cost to government in first year of Prohibition: $280 million in lost tax revenues plus cost of running federal enforcement effort.
1927	Production of malt syrups and extracts used in homebrewing reaches 888 million pounds; major grocery chains feature large displays of malt syrup for customers.
1930	Great Depression begins; call for repeal of prohibition grows.
1933	Volstead Act repealed and 23rd Amendment passes. On April 7, Prohibition repealed and beer brewed legally in America for the first time in 13 years.
1934	751 breweries open after Repeal; most ever after Prohibition. Federal government enacts numerous regulations on brewing. "Tied houses" regulations prevent breweries from operating retail outlets or saloons.

1935	Metal container for holding beverages invented; beer put in cans for first time.
1940	Six breweries producing 1 million barrels/year (Anheuser-Busch, Schlitz, Pabst, Ballantine, Schaefer, Ruppert).
1942	Breweries join war effort; key brewery workers granted deferments; women go to work in breweries.
1943	Government rations barley malt; breweries restricted to 93% of barley used previous year. Result is thinner beer.
1945	W.W. II ends, brewery production highest in history: 80 million barrels/year, up from 53 million in 1940.
1960s	Era of brewery mergers and consolidations; fewer than 50 breweries in U.S.
1965	Fritz Maytag purchases San Francisco's Anchor brewery; brews steam beer and registers patent on name.
1977	Californian Jack McAuliffe opens New Albion, first micro-brewery, in Sonoma.
1979	Phillip Morris acquires Miller Brewing; brewery takeovers begin; Justice Department Antritrust Division studies situation, issues report.
	Public Law 95-458 passes; homebrewing legal again in U.S.; any adult can brew up to 100 gallons per year.
1982	Bert Grant opens America's first brewpub, Yakima Brewing and Malting, Yakima, Washington.
	California changes law, permits brewpubs.
1983	California's first two brewpubs open: Buffalo Bill's in Hayward, Mendocino Brewing in Hopland.
1984	17 microbreweries and brewpubs open in one year in U.S.
1985	Matthew Reich opens "New Amsterdam Brewery and Taproom" in Manhattan; first full-scale microbrewery and brewpub in U.S.
1986	Samuel Adams wins Most Popular Beer in America for the second straight year at the Great American Beer Festival.
	55 microbreweries and brewpubs operating.

A DICTIONARY OF BEER

ALE — a type of beer fermented at higher temperatures (60-75 degrees F) with top fermenting yeast *(Saccharomyces cerevisiae)*. During fermentation, ale yeast gathers at the top of the vessel where it can be skimmed and used again. Ale is usually darker and "hoppier" than lagers which are brewed at lower temperatures with bottom fermenting yeast. Ales tend to have yeasty aromas and flavors.

Ales historically were the most popular beer from early civilizations up to the mid-19th century. English-style ales were the preferred beer in America from the time of Pilgrims in the early 1600s to the 1840s when German immigrants introduced lager beer.

BARREL — One U.S. barrel equals 31 gallons (1.17 hectoliters). The common unit of production used by breweries. Early beer was brewed in oaken barrels; today, brewing is done in stainless steel tanks.

BLACK PATENT MALT— malted barley roasted at high temperatures until the grain is black and toasted. Used in porter and stout beers.

BOTTOM FERMENTING — lager yeast *(Saccharomyces carlsbergensis)* that ferments sugars at the bottom of the fermenting vessel (where it falls out after fermentation is completed) at lower temperatures (32-50 degrees F). Fermenting with lager yeast takes longer due to lower temperatures.

BOUQUET — the aromatic smell associated with hop flowers added to beer during brewing. Hop "nose" will depend upon the hops used and their aromatic properties. Esters from fermentation and malt also contribute to a beer's bouquet.

CARAMEL MALT — malted barley which has been heated until sugars crystalize within the grain. Adds golden color to beer and slight sweetness. Used in both ales and lagers.

CASK CONDITIONING — English ales delivered to pubs with yeast still working in the cask. The yeast is allowed to settle for several days so the ale can reach prime conditioning in the cask before being served.

DEXTRIN — complex sugars that are not fermented by yeast in brewing. These unfermented sugars make a beer fuller and more flavorful.

ESTERS — aromatic flavors generated by yeast metabolism. Beers can give off such esters or aromas as strawberry, apple, banana, or grapefruit. An "estery" nose caused by higher fermentation temperature is characteristic of English ales but not of lager beers.

ETHANOL — or ethyl alcohol, the consumable alcohol produced by the fermentation of sugars by yeast. The alcohol in beer.

FININGS — a material which removes haziness in fermented beer but does not remain in the finished beer. Irish moss (seaweed), isinglass or gelatin are finings which clarify beer.

GRIST — crushed barley malt; added with hot water in mash tun to produce wort.

HOPS — a climbing plant, *Humulus lupulus,* in the cannabis family which produces flowery cones. The cones contain tannins that preserve beer and oils and resins that give an aroma and dryness to beer. Hops are added during the boiling of wort to achieve the desired bitterness and aroma. Hops are grown in the Northwest, particularly in Washington's Yakima Valley, and in select regions of Europe and the British Isles. The types of hops are varied and important in the taste and smell of beer. Common hop types are Cascade, Clusters, Fuggles, Saaz, Hallertauer, Tettnanger, Northern Brewer and Goldings.

HOP EXTRACT — hops syrup or pellets extracted from hop flowers for homebrewing or specialty brewing. Some larger breweries use hop extract to produce cheaper beer.

KRAUSEN — a technique developed by early German brewers to add a small amount of unfermented wort to the fermented beer as it is run into the closed conditioning tank. The unfermented wort provides additional sugars for the yeast to ferment and to carbonate the beer. Many microbreweries use krausening to produce smoother lager beer.

LAGER — type of beer brewed at low temperatures (32-50 degrees F) with lager yeast *(Saccharomyces carlsbergensis)* that works at the bottom of the fermenting vessel. Lager originated in the Central Europe nations of Germany, Austria and Czechoslovakia and quickly spread throughout the world in the 19th century.

Lager is the most popular style of beer in the world. Lager beers include Bock, Maibock, Pilsner, Vienna, Marzen and Munich beers.

MALTOSE — simple sugar produced from the blend of hot water and malted barley which later is fermented to produce alcohol.

PASTEURIZATION — the process of heating a liquid to kill living organisms. Beer that has been pasteurized has had wild yeast or bacteria killed along with the fermentation yeast. Pasteurization permits beer to be shipped or stored without the risk of contamination. Non-pasteurized beer in not "unhealthy" by any means; it merely has a small amount of fermenting yeast still working.

PRIMARY FERMENTATION — the vigorous fermentation that takes place when yeast is added to wort. Yeast ferments simple sugars into carbon dioxide and alcohol.

SECONDARY FERMENTATION — more subdued fermentation that takes place in casks or tanks when the beer is stored or "lagered." Carbonation, clarification and flavor stabilization occur during secondary fermentation.

SKUNKY — a disagreeable aroma and harsh taste frequently found in beers stored in green bottles. Skunky beer has been "light-struck" by the sun's ultraviolet light which penetrates through clear or green glass. Beer bottled in brown glass is one protection against "skunkiness."

TOP FERMENTING — the process used to ferment ale using *Saccharomyces cerevisiae* yeast and brewing at high temperatures (60-75 degrees F).

WATER — the best water a brewery can use is that which requires no special treatment. Many breweries in Europe and America have a sole source of mountain water which they claim as the reason for the "purity" of their beer. Any treated public source of water is good enough for a brewery as long as chlorine is removed.

WILD YEAST — present in air and soil; can cause undesirable flavors and aroma in beer when brewing does not follow strict standards of cleanliness. Some Belgian and German beers brew with wild yeast, frequently producing a wine-like taste.

WORT — (pronounced "wert") the sweet liquid resulting from the blend of hot water and malted barley. "Sweet wort" is produced at the beginning of brewing; it becomes "bitter wort" after it is boiled and hops are added. When yeast is pitched and fermentation begins, wort becomes beer.

YEAST — the critical catalyst in fermenting beer. Top fermenting yeast *(Saccharomyces cerevisiae)* works at warmer temperatures (60-75 degrees F) and drifts to the top of the fermenting vessel to produce ales, porters, stout, Altbier and wheat beers. Top fermented beers are better served at warmer temperatures (55 degrees F). Many ale yeasts are hybrids of blends which have evolved in various brewhouses.

Bottom fermenting yeast *(Saccharomyces carlsbergensis)* works at cooler temperatures (40-55 degrees F) after which the beer is chilled (32-38 degrees F) for several weeks to produce a crisp, clear lager. Lagers are better served at colder temperatures (40-50 degrees F). Lager yeasts are usually "scientifically pure" and produce a consistent style of beer.

★   ★   ★

BIBLIOGRAPHY

Although there are a few magazines, newsletters and books on beer, the choice of publications is not as diverse or up-to-date as it should be. Certainly, when compared with the variety of publications about wine — including American wines — the literature on beer pales by comparison.

It is puzzling why newspapers and magazines cover wine and food yet almost ignore beer in modern American cuisine. This oversight may be attributed to the lack of variety in beer brewed by industrial brewers. But since the 1970s when imported beer became popular and micro-brewed beers appeared, the choice of beers available in restaurants, supermarkets and liquor stores has improved dramatically. Although magazines and newspapers have observed the trend, it has been more out of curiosity than any attempt to treat it seriously. Their attitude seems to be, "That's interesting that there are these new microbreweries, but what could be significant about something as common as beer?"

That cavalier approach is a mistake.

Beer is a food enjoyed by 80 million American men and women of all backgrounds, cultures and interests. The history and origins of beer are as rich and colorful as any food. Beer is a nutritious beverage that can have as many tastes and delights as there are colors to observe.

In simple terms, beer does not have the "respect" it deserves, partially because it has been linked to the working class and the common man. But no more; beer is coming of age and people are realizing their choice in beer is not limited to light lagers but to a gourmet's selection of rich tastes and varieties from across the country and around the world.

It's good now, but it's going to get a lot better. One objective of this book is to spur interest among the general public and the media to pay attention to the changes going on in the American beer market. The changes are significant; they portend an exciting future for anyone interested in beer and its place in the cultural and culinary history of the nation.

PERIODICALS

"All About Beer." Bimonthly publication of McMullen Publishing, 2145 W. La Palma Avenue, Anaheim, California 92801. A general magazine on what's happening in the beer world.

"Beer Marketer's Insights." Jerry Steinman, 55 Virginia Avenue, West Nyack, New York. Semimonthly newsletter containing statistics and news on the brewing industry. An insider's view of marketing, sales and production in brewing.

"The Grist." 2 Balfour Road, London, N5, England. Bimonthly trade magazine for small breweries in North America, England, Australia and New Zealand. Publishes technical articles on all phases of small-scale brewing.

"Amateur Brewer." Box 713, Hayward, California 94543-0713. In 1985, "Home Fermenters Digest" bought Fred Eckhardt's "Amateur Brewer" and adopted its name. Published by Bill Owens, owner of Buffalo Bill's Microbrewery, one of the country's first brewpubs.

"Listen to Your Beer." Amateur Brewer Information Service, P.O. Box 546, Portland, Oregon 97207. Quarterly publication of Fred Eckhardt, a colorful and well-known beer writer who writes a column for the Portland "Oregonian."

"The New Brewer." Association of Brewers, Box 287, Boulder, Colorado 80306-0287. Telephone: (303) 447-0816. All the news in the microbrewing and brewpub worlds. The Association is a branch of the American Homebrewers Association.

"On Tap." Ben Novak, Centre Daily Times, State College, Pennsylvania. Novak's bimonthly column has been running since September 1984, and features articles about specialty beers of the world and the social history of beer and brewing. Novak is a lawyer who writes like a philosopher.

"What's Brewing." The Campaign for Real Ale (CAMRA), 34 Alma Street, St. Albans, Hertfordshire, England, AL 1 3 BW. Monthly newsletter by the non-profit group that started the microbrewing revolution in England.

"World Beer Review." WBR Publications, P.O. Box 71, Clemson, South Carolina 29633. A new entry into the world of beer newsletters, featuring up-to-date information on beers from around the world. Published monthly.

"Zymurgy." American Homebrewers Association, Box 287, Boulder, Colorado. Editor-in-chief, Charlie Papazian. A five-times yearly guide written by and for homebrewers. An excellent source for anyone interested in the popular hobby of homebrewing. Many microbrewers began as homebrewers and became entrepreneurs.

BOOKS

Anderson, Will. "Beer, USA." Dobbs Ferry, New York: Morgan & Morgan, Inc. 1986. An informal documentary of chronological anecdotes in the history of beer in America. Anderson has published several books on beer; this one documents a nostalgic trip he took through the Midwest to capture the common man's story of beer. The photos Anderson collected from libraries and brewery archives capture an era earlier in this century when almost every town had a brewery and a Saturday night "beer party" and dance brought together a community of all ages and types. The photos are extraordinarily vivid and memorable.

Asbury, Herbert. "The Great Illusion: An Informal History of Prohibition." Garden City, New York: Doubleday & Company, 1950. An excellent treatment of temperance movements in America and "The Noble Experiment" that they created in the 1920s and '30s.

Baron, Stanley. "Brewed in America: A History of Beer and Ale in the United States." Boston: Little, Brown & Co., 1962. A comprehensive history of brewing in America from the early colonists to the mid-20th century.

Bickerdyke, John. "The Curiousities of Ale & Beer." London: Spring Books, 1889. A wonderful and humorous collection of old drinking songs, ballads, sagas and doggerel about drinking and good fellowship. A treasure.

Cottone, Vince. "Good Beer Guide: Breweries and Pubs of the Pacific Northwest, British Columbia, Washington and Oregon." Seattle: Homestead Book Company, 1986. An excellent and timely book documenting the Northwest microbrewing revolution. Included is a guide to pubs, taverns and restaurants that carry specialty beers. Similar format to the CAMRA Good Beer Guides published annually in England.

"Campaign for Real Ale Good Beer Guide." London: Annual publication of the English CAMRA organization working to bring back real ale to England. Presents a guide to nearly 200 breweries in England and the 6,000 pubs which serve real ale. Well illustrated, includes maps.

Ford, Gene. "Ford's Illustrated Guide to Wines, Brews & Spirits." Dubuque, Iowa: Wm. C. Brown Publishers, 1983. A comprehensive view of the history, culture, and production of all spirits. Excellent treatment of beer and brewing. Richly illustrated.

Hillman, Howard. "The Gourmet Guide to Beer." New York: Washington Square Press, 1983. A rating of beers of the world.

Jackson, Michael. "The Pocket Guide to Beer." New York: G.P. Putnam, (A Perigree Book), 1982. A short version of Jackson's classic World Guide to Beer.

--------. "The Simon and Schuster Pocket Guide to Beer." New York: Simon and Schuster (A Fireside Book), 1986. The title explains the book. Simon and Schuster wanted a pocket guide to beer with their name in the title as if Jackson's name weren't enough to sell the book. The book is as thin as a bottle cap and contains only a fraction of what Jackson could have written. This slim volume's only redeeming feature is that it can be slipped into the vest pocket or purse of a traveler exploring the world of beer. They'll learn a few names of famous breweries and beers, but without the depth or sophistication the subject merits.

--------. "The World Guide to Beer." Philadelphia: Running Press, 1977. The classic book on beer. Very well designed with charts, graphs, illustrations and pictures of breweries — past and present — from all over the world. It will be years before any comparable book will be written with the level of knowledge and affection that Jackson presents here.

Mares, William. "Making Beer." New York: Alfred A. Knopf, 1984. A Vermont journalist's tale of how his homebrewing passion almost led him to start a microbrewery. Required reading for anyone seriously considering becoming a microbrewer.

"Microbrewers Resource Handbook and Directory: 1986." Boulder: Brewers Publications; compiled by the Institute for Fermentation and Brewing Studies, 1986. An up-to-date directory of microbrewers, pubbrewers, suppliers, manufacturers and consultants. Excellent resource for potential microbrewers or serious students of brewing.

Papazian, Charlie. "The Complete Joy of Home Brewing." New York: Avon, 1984. Papazian is president of the American Homebrewers Association and one of the most knowledgeable people about the microbrewing revolution. An excellent and easy-to-read guide for first-time brewers and veteran homebrewers.

Robertson, James. "The Great American Beer Book." Ottawa, Illinois and Thorwood, New York: Caroline House, 1978.

Steinman, Jerry. "The Beer Industry: A Comprehensive Review and Analysis." West Nyack, N.Y., 1982. Statistics on the production and sales of American breweries.

--------. "1986 Beer Industry Update: A Review of Recent Developments." West Nyack, New York, 1986.

Weiner, Michael A. "The Taster's Guide to Beer: Beers and Breweries of the World." New York: MacMillan Publishing Co., 1977. Beer around the world.

Yenne, Bill. "Beers of North America." New York: Gallery Books, 1986. Beer and breweries from the Caribbean Islands and Yucatan to Milwaukee, St. Louis, British Columbia and Ontario. A coffee table book filled with color photos and labels of breweries operating throughout North America.

"100 Years of Brewing: A Complete History of the Progress Made in the Art, Science and Industry of Brewing in the World, Particularly in the 19th Century." Chicago & New York: H.S. Rich & Company,

1903. Lists thousands of breweries operating during the "Golden Age" of brewing before the temperance movement and mergers thinned the ranks. Even a casual browsing through the massive study lends an appreciation of how significant brewing was to the national economy in the 19th century and the role it played in developing our cultural heritage.

★   ★   ★

Index

Postscript

I hope that reading "Star Spangled Beer" was an entertaining and informative look for you into the world of microbrewing; it certainly was to write it.

Even as this book was going to press, I was laying the groundwork to write an expanded history and directory on microbrewing (tentative publication date: Summer 1989) that will incorporate the many changes going on throughout the industry. Although it is too early to say what those changes will be, I believe they will include many more microbreweries, far more brewpubs, a wider selection of beers and much greater public awareness about specialty beers.

I also believe that the next 10 years will become, in some fashion, the "Decade of Beer" as more Americans and Canadians rediscover our historical and cultural links to brewing and become more involved — whether by trying more specialty beers, reading about brewing and beer styles, demanding more than just industrial brewed light lager, and maybe even trying a little homebrewing. The result will be an increased awareness and appreciation for beer.

This does not mean we will return to the time when every town or neighborhood had a brewery; instead, consumers will find much greater choice in the beer marketplace and maybe even will visit a brewpub or microbrewery and drink beer they way it should be drunk — fresh from the brewery and brimming with rich flavors and aromas.

In time, microbrewed beers may rival imports in popularity and sales, and it won't be unusual to go to a party or sit in a restaurant and hear people debate beer as passionately and knowledgeably as they once did wine or cheese. With this thought in mind, I would like to ask readers to keep me in mind when the topic of beer comes up. If you are just becoming aware of microbrewed beers, let me know how you discovered them, which ones you liked (and disliked) and what you are looking for in specialty beers. If microbrewed beers are not new to you, I would like to know your experiences as well.

What I am really asking is for readers of "Star Spangled Beer" to become a part of my next book on microbrewing. That book will include a chapter on consumers' response to microbrewed beers and will quote from your letters and cards.

Another chapter in that book will rate beers. This rating will not say, "This is the best beer brewed in America," or anything as presumptuous; rather, the rating will include many beers and list those considered the best in various categories. For example, the Best Amber Beer may include three: Pale Ales six, Porters four. One final ranking, however, will say: "These are the best beers currently being brewed in America." That list may include two, or five or eight, and include several styles; it's too early to tell.

To conduct this rating, I will once again be visiting microbreweries and brewpubs across the U.S. and Canada. I will taste beer fresh at the brewery but I'll also sample them away from the brewery since that will more accurately reflect what you, the consumer, are getting in the marketplace.

So . . . as you go about exploring the world of microbrewed beers, remember that your opinions are important. I am interested in them . . . so are the microbrewers . . . and everyone else who is discovering specialty beers and wants to exchange opinions.

If you would like to get on a mailing list to receive information about "Star Spangled Beer II" (I guarantee the title of the book will be more original than that), write a card or letter and mention that you want to receive a pre-publication announcement. I'll be sure that you do.

Please write to:

> "Star Spangled Beer" Consumer Poll
> or
> "Star Spangled Beer II"
> (for pre-publication announcement)
> RedBrick Press
> P.O. Box 2184
> Reston, VA 22090

Thanks for reading "Star Spangled Beer."

Jack Erickson
Reston, Virginia
March 11, 1987

Yes, I would like to order a copy of "Star Spangled Beer" to learn about the exciting new world of microbrewing and brewpubs.

I am enclosing $13.95 for each copy, plus $1.50 for shipping.

"Star Spangled Beer"
RedBrick Press
P.O. Box 2184
Reston, VA 22090

Name _____ Phone _____

Address _____

City _____ State _____ Zip _____

Yes, I would like to order a copy of "Star Spangled Beer" to learn about the exciting new world of microbrewing and brewpubs.

I am enclosing $13.95 for each copy, plus $1.50 for shipping.

"Star Spangled Beer"
RedBrick Press
P.O. Box 2184
Reston, VA 22090

Name _____ Phone _____

Address _____

City _____ State _____ Zip _____

Yes, I would like to order a copy of "Star Spangled Beer" to learn about the exciting new world of microbrewing and brewpubs.

I am enclosing $13.95 for each copy, plus $1.50 for shipping.

"Star Spangled Beer"
RedBrick Press
P.O. Box 2184
Reston, VA 22090

Name _____ Phone _____

Address _____

City _____ State _____ Zip _____